MW00717092

AUDACIOUS
FAITH

A Little Slice of Heaven

Darnette Hill

God Bless,

Mary F. Woodruff

Mary Fannie Burton Woodruff — Woodruff's Café & Pie Shop, 2016

A Little Slice of Heaven

A Celebration of Faith, Family, Perseverance, and Pie

Angela Woodruff Scott

First Printing 2017

Audacious Faith, LLC : Publishers

The Good Books People

www.GoodBooks.us

Audacious Faith, LLC www.GoodBooks.us
Published by Audacious Faith, LLC—Publishers.
Editing, Design, Photography & Illustrations by
Donald A. Garlock, Jr. for Audacious Faith, LLC.
Additional photographs courtesy of the
Woodruff Family Collection. Used by permission.

Printed in the United States of America. First Printing.

Publisher's Cataloging-in-Publication data:

Scott, Angela Woodruff, 1959—
A Little Slice of Heaven : A Celebration of Faith, Family, Perseverance, and Pie / Angela Woodruff Scott.
p. cm.
Includes index.
Hardcover:
ISBN-13: 978-0-9982389-0-6
Paperback:
ISBN-13: 978-0-9982389-1-3
E-PUB:
ISBN-13: 978-0-9982389-2-0
E-PDF:
ISBN-13: 978-0-9982389-3-7

1. Family—US_History—Slavery—Virginia—Inspiration—Anecdotes.
2. Woodruff's Store. Woodruff's Café & Pie Shop. History. Virginia. Amherst County, Virginia.
I. Title.

for Mama

in memory of Daddy

Contents

Oh, taste and see

that the Lord is good;

— Psalm 34:8a

For My yoke is easy

and My burden

is light.

— Matthew 11:30

Foreword

I OFTEN SAY THAT MY FAVORITE PART of aging is perspective. That's another way of saying, "If I had known then what I know now...", to which the obvious retort is, "Just what is it that you know now?" One thing I know now is that everything a teacher does is noticed, and one never knows the impact of the slightest gesture.

I frequently find myself running into former students and am sometimes surprised by the things they tell me. Occasionally, their particular memories of the simplest things hardly seem to warrant remembering 40 years later.

Probably the first time I stopped in Woodruff's Store, Angie and I recalled school days, from the early 1970s, and she said, "When I was in the 8th grade, we had a talent show, and I was singing and was really nervous. You encouraged me so much. It really was important to me and I still remember it." I was happy to know I'd done something right, but, of course, singing isn't my forte at all; I taught Angie in the gym. But it was important to her at the time, and it's meaningful to me now. It was Angie Woodruff who was teaching the lesson.

When Angie re-opened Woodruff's Store, I became a frequent customer. It was a convenient lunch, and I enjoyed visiting at Mrs. Woodruff's table. I would tell her that I came in for the entertainment. I tried to encourage others to stop by, and now feel some satisfaction in contributing to the success. Where else could one bring his dog for curb service, as "Molly" and "Jack" enjoyed their weekly trip for a hot dog, cut into bite-size pieces and often fed to them in the parking lot by the proprietor?

As a regular, I grew to know the others, to the point that I started suggesting to Angie that if we were good enough writers, we should be able to turn our experiences into a TV show. We had all the components with the cast of diverse characters, with emphasis on "characters." We had various members of the Woodruff family, plus a couple of doctors, a lawyer, woodcutters, hunters, laborers, teachers, housewives, a minister, retirees, and complete strangers. Somebody occasionally would show up with a 35-pound cabbage from his garden. We had a lot of laughs, and, even if there were no story, we could certainly create one.

Mrs. Woodruff is always good for a memorable turn of phrase. About the two medical people, she cited one, "Now he doesn't *look* like a doctor," as quoted elsewhere in this book. About the other, retired and faithfully working in his nearby vineyard, while maintaining his professional bearing and distinguished appearance, she proclaimed, "Now, Jim, he looks like he *used to be somebody.*" We don't hesitate to remind Jim that in Mrs. Woodruff's eyes, he used to be somebody, but we're withholding judgment on his current status.

I would occasionally come racing into the store to tell Angie about a word somebody had misspelled on her sign, because we had agreed that it didn't reflect well on her. I think I brought her up short one day when I told her that "your ampersand is backwards." She didn't know whether she needed to change her sign or put on more clothes. It became our little joke, if somebody's ampersand was backwards.

We regulars have taken pleasure in Woodruff's newfound fame, commencing with the *Southern Living* piece, followed by numerous features on local television, in newspapers across the state, and even in the PBS special. We have marveled at the people from far-flung places who have stopped after having seen one of the promotions. I take note of license plates in the parking lot, and am quick to say, "Which one of you rode a motorcycle from California today just for lunch?" Once, a man whose accent I didn't recognize identified himself as being from Australia, and I welcomed him, "That's a long way to come for a slice of pie."

But, regardless of the circumstances, the one constant at Woodruff's Store, of course, is Mrs. Woodruff. She has greeted customers for decades. As illustrated so clearly in this book, nobody has ever been turned away from her hospitality, with perhaps the exception of the would-be flimflammers as described herein.

The Woodruffs and extended family have weathered change, but have maintained a strong and steady sense of integrity, benevolence, and fair play, irrespective of the situation. The history of the Woodruff family parallels that of this country. Personal, societal and economic upheaval occurs, predictably or not, on both small and large scales, personally or nationally, yet the principles by which the Woodruffs live and work remain as well-defined as a century ago. With an unwavering foundation of faith and strong leadership, they have exhibited a clear vision of who they are, where they want to go, and how they intend to get there. And they know that the rewards will be self-evident.

As we Americans experience what seem to be turbulent times, we could learn vital lessons from practicing what occurs in Woodruff's Store. One would be hard-pressed to find a place more welcoming or just plain American. He will leave not only with food that will "stick to his ribs," but also will have been part of something greater—an experience with people who are working hard to provide for customers, making no excuses for difficulties, being grateful for what has come their way, and perhaps leading in singing a favorite hymn. They readily face the next challenge, even if it's a dozen pies that somebody wants finished by yesterday.

As Mary Woodruff enjoys her 100th year, we continue to reap the glories of her wisdom. Among my favorite quotes from recent days, as I expectantly awaited the pronouncement, is, "Leah, you know, if you live long enough... you're going to get old." We're not noticing any evidence of that yet, though. There are many more lessons to be taught and pies to be enjoyed.

— Leah Settle Gibbs

AMHERST COUNTY, VIRGINIA

1 OCTOBER 2016

WOODRUFF'S
STORE

Prologue

"WHAT'S THAT SMELL? I SMELL *SMOKE!*" I shouted as I ran back toward the kitchen. "Larry! Larry, the *kitchen's* on fire!" The awful smell of burning oil, hot metal, and melting plastic billowed from the smoke-filled kitchen. The curtains were alight with flames that shot toward the ceiling. The stove was melting. The clock on the wall was dripping globs of molten plastic as if it were in a Salvador Dali painting. We coughed and choked and waved our arms for the nearest fire extinguisher. Squinting through burning eyes, we put the fire out, and opened every window in the building. As we stumbled outside and caught our breath, we talked to the firemen who were armed with not only a fire hose, but questions. And then, of course, Mama showed up to witness the spectacle. It wasn't pretty.

I blamed myself. I was so tired, and others saw it. They were trying to help me hold onto this dream, which frankly hadn't been going well at all. When the tumult had died and the smoke had cleared, we quickly ordered a new stove. Larry got some paint and covered the blackened walls and ceiling with a fresh coat of white. Soon we were back with at least the appearance of normalcy, but I was still tired, and I felt like giving up.

It wasn't the first time. After all, according to the experts, we had done everything wrong, anyway. Nine out of ten restaurants fail in their first year, don't they? We didn't have a wad of cash. We didn't have a prime location. We didn't have fancy equipment. We didn't have a marketing budget. Other than working in the food service industry, I had no idea how to run a business. People, *including* my husband, told me that I was crazy to want to open up a café. Especially in the unpretentious 1951 two-story cinderblock building built out in the country by my Daddy. The same old building had housed not only my family, but Mama's country cash grocery store for 30 years: Woodruff's Store. Even they closed down, didn't they? All of the odds seemed stacked against it from the start.

I lay awake in bed that night pondering how close we had come to losing the entire business, the entire building. I was grateful to God that no one was hurt and He had spared the Shop. But I was beyond exhausted. And I started questioning myself: "What was I thinking when I opened this Shop?" "Was I being selfish—holding on so tightly to this crazy dream?" and "How in the world did we get here?"

My mind kept drifting back over my family. What right did I, as the baby of the family, have to question what had brought me to this place? My siblings had grown up here, and my parents, and their parents, too, and life certainly hadn't been easy for any of them. I just couldn't give up.

Everyone was watching me. Would quitting be smart, or would I be letting them down?

There is a legacy handed down through the generations and tied to this Corner too strong to be denied. So, I'd like to share with you some snapshots of my family. Some of these glimpses are tragic, some riveting, some divine, still others downright hilarious. But they're all true, and just like the ingredients in a recipe that comes together, they blend perfectly to tell the story of why we are still here.

To be sure, our Mama, celebrity centenarian that she is this year—and a force to be reckoned with—is one of the main ingredients. And Daddy, who has been gone for 18 years now, remains an inspiration to us all.

But time and again my mind drifts back to an enslaved man, born about 1832 and right around the corner, who held tight to his faith and his hope.

That slave's name was Wyatt Woodruff.

He was our great-grandfather.

— Angela Woodruff Scott
Agricola, Virginia
1 October 2016

WOODRUFF'S
Coca-Cola
STORE
Coca-Cola

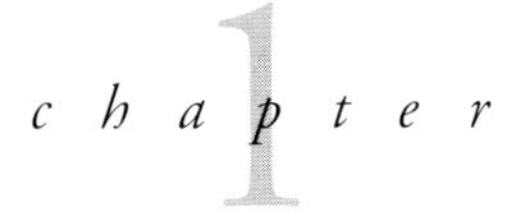

The Corner Blacksmith

When Wyatt's mother gave birth to him about 1832 in Amherst County, Virginia, the joy over this new life was mingled with sorrow, for Wyatt had been born into bondage. Slavery was all Wyatt's parents had ever known, and their hopes for something better for their baby boy were fairly dim. They couldn't have known that a corner of the county would become known for generations to come as Wyatt's Corner—a name synonymous with hospitality for miles around.

Family lore is supported by documents, such as 19th-century U.S. Census records and "Slave Schedules," as they were called. These schedules reduced enslaved humanity to a number on a tally sheet for taxation purposes, listing only the sex and age of each enslaved person under the name of the owner.

All indications are that Wyatt was owned by a family by the name of Woodruff. It was not uncommon for slaves to be given or to assume a surname. He was later sold to a slave owner by the name of Nathan Rucker, who was actually four years younger. Nathan and Wyatt were both born at Salt Creek (which never seemed to have a population of more than two dozen people), and they might well have been acquaintances, if not playmates. Still, it was to Nathan whom Wyatt belonged when the War Between the States erupted. It is not known precisely when Wyatt became a free man—whether by the Emancipation Proclamation in the midst of the War (1863), or during or after his service in the 15th U.S. Colored Infantry as a breastworks man. (Breastworks were earthen fortifications that required fast-and-furious digging by hand and the mounding of walls. Here in central Virginia, many of these earthen defenses are visible to this day.)

We know for certain that Wyatt survived the War and emerged a free man with a pension of $\$12.^{50}$ per month and worked as a blacksmith for a prominent local farmer by the name of Thomas Townley, who owned a tan yard and a blacksmith shop. With the money he had earned, Wyatt purchased the blacksmith operation from Mr. Townley, and set up shop on the corner of what are now called Elon Road and East Perch Road.

In the center of the section of the 1864 map, drawn in exacting detail by the Confederate Army Corps of Engineers for the benefit of their troops, one can clearly see landmarks that have been home to the Woodruffs for generations. Villages and towns are in all caps. Small squares pinpoint households with the surname of the family that lived there. We can clearly see Salt Creek with the Tan Yard on its bank, and three occurrences of the name Rucker. At the foot of Tobacco Row Mountain, find the

Section of an 1864 Map of Amherst County, Virginia, showing Elon and environs, including the James River, the Tan Yard on Salt Creek, and Tobacco Row Mountain. Library of Congress, Geography and Map Division.

"n" in the surname of John. That is the precise location of Wyatt's blacksmith shop. That's Wyatt's Corner. That's our Corner. That's *Home*.

We are not aware of any photos of Wyatt, but we do have some treasured relics from his shop: tools he made for his own use, including this blacksmith's shovel.

Not only was Wyatt Woodruff now a free man and a landowner, he had just become—officially—the first black business owner ever in Amherst County, Virginia.

We know from church records that the folks of the formerly enslaved community around here wasted little time in organizing. For generations, they had to pray to the Almighty for their freedom in secret. And so it was with great excitement and grateful hearts that, in September of 1866, they met openly under a grape arbor in a small pasture about a quarter-mile down from the Corner, where they convened to organize their church and plan for a new meeting house, rather than the old tobacco barn they had used for years.

Among those present were their first pastor, the Rev. W. J. Lewis; deacon Westly Green; Wyatt Woodruff and his son, Walter, a deacon; French Turner; James Miller; Henry Singleton; David Ware; Charles Brown; William Johnson; Nancy Huckstep; Carolina Eubanks; Nancy Trimble; Betsy Jones; Charlotte Jackson, and many others under the direction of the Rev. Sampson White of Lynchburg. Some decades later, for an observance of this historic occasion, Martha Green was preparing a speech, scribbling her longhand in a Red Top brand pencil tablet. Martha had married Daddy's cousin, Ottie, a fellow grandson of blacksmith Wyatt. She held a teaching certificate, was the church secretary, and had become the church historian. This was her introduction:

> *Prayer is the soul's sincere desire, unuttered or expressed, the motion of a hidden fire that trembles on the breast. Slavery's prayer was sincere, but could not be uttered in words as it can today, and the very desire for its utterance made individuals tremble, cry, shout, and sing in secret. But when God changed condition of affairs in 1865, and declared slavery should exist no longer, secret prayer was no longer needed, and on the third Lord's Day of September of 1866, a few of those old faithful patriots organized themselves into the Chestnut Grove Baptist Church of Amherst County, Virginia.*

By the time the U.S. census taker rolled around to this neck of the woods in July of 1870, Wyatt was no longer on a "Slave Schedule" as a piece of property listed only by gender and age, but was a landowner and a business owner. The horrors and hardships of the so-called Reconstruction period are for another book, but Wyatt and his family seem to have done well during this time, and he gradually increased the size of his property around Wyatt's Corner, particularly if a family had a need to sell. In his time, this Corner was known to travelers between the Forks of Buffalo and Lynchburg as a place where they could stop and rest, water their horses, and camp for the night without charge.

Wyatt the blacksmith, about 37 in 1870, was living on this Corner with his wife, Sarah (better known as Sally), 28, and five children: James J. (15), Rebecca (14), Emma (12), Mary (3), and David (about 7 months old). The census taker carefully filled in the race column, along with the columns he checked off for each family member: "cannot read," and "cannot write."

By the time the Census was taken again in June of 1880, the two eldest children, James and Rebecca, had moved on, and the youngest, David, born on the first of December 1868, had died sometime in the interim decade. But Wyatt and Sally had added five more children to their nest: Thomas, 9, Silas, 6, Wesley, 5, Paulus, 3, and Walter, age 2.

This youngest of ten offspring, Walter Nathaniel Woodruff, born the 3rd day of May 1878 (when Wyatt was about 46), would grow up to become our grandfather. Daddy's dad. We called him "Papa." We kids remember him as being a strong, independent, somewhat stern man. Still, he had a heart for people, and instilled in his children the qualities that endure. After all, it was at his repeated urging that his son, our Daddy, began building in 1951 what started out as a shelter from the elements for school kids waiting for the bus, and became our home and the corner store and a place of refuge for more people than anyone could ever have anticipated.

Here's a fascinating side note about one of our clan who caused quite a stir around Salt Creek: Around the turn of the 20th century, most of Walter's siblings moved away from Salt Creek, and some of them landed in Pennsylvania. Brother Silas (four years older than Walter), and his wife Sally, reared a family of 12 children in Connellsville, just this side of Pittsburgh. One of those 12 was named John, who became known as "Long John" for his 6'3" stature and long stride. John was a fellow teammate of Jesse Owens on the U.S. Olympic team for the 1936 games in Berlin. John won the gold medal—right under the nose of Adolf Hitler—for a remarkable win in the 800 meters with what has been called "the most daring move ever made on track," and much has been written about it. Let's just say that there is more than a little family pride over what cousin John accomplished.

Meanwhile, unlike his siblings, Walter was the only one of Wyatt's offspring who stayed close to home, and he and his wife, Aurelia (née Watkins), had married on 27 August 1902. Our Daddy, James, was their fourth child. After Wyatt's passing, Walter bought out the shares of Wyatt's estate from his siblings.

Walter's wife, Aurelia, was born on the 4th of April 1881, daughter of Reuben and Thora Watkins. Early in 1930, Aurelia was riding in a car driven by our Dad, who was then 17. When another driver cut him off, Daddy swerved and wrecked the car, with Aurelia suffering a broken back, and languishing in a body cast for some time before passing away on the 6th of July 1930 at the age of 49. Daddy never spoke of the accident, or his dear mother, again. We think he blamed himself for the tragedy. Walter never married again. He continued to visit with his four children, and planted gardens and raised chickens. In his later years, Walter became disabled and was confined to a wheelchair. He lived with our family until he died at age 84 on the 20th of January 1968.

The Burtons

Our Mama, Mary Fannie, was born a Burton, and they hailed from Salt Creek, about a mile down from the Corner on East Perch Road on the north bank of the James River. As Mama tells it, she was the sixth of ten children born to Henry and Hattie Burton. Seven boys and three girls. "Papa Henry," as we called him, was born in 1877, and "Grandma Hattie" in 1882.

Mama's large family lived in an old three-story house with outbuildings, such as a hen house and other necessaries of a family farm. We call it the Home House, and it was command central for all Homecomers. It was a wonderful, magical place to be!

There was always the smell of good food being prepared. The dirt floor basement held the stores of homemade wine and vegetables that Grandma had laboriously canned from the season's bounty. Grandma Hattie grew up one of 10 kids, and never even knew who her father was. She gave birth to 10 kids of her own. She knew hard work and she loved to make people happy, especially with food, lovingly and expertly prepared. She was always making something in the kitchen, baking bread, peach cobblers, sweet potato pies, fried pies and more. She always had meals ready for her children and, later, her granchildren. With their ten children and extended families, one can imagine what a busy place it was.

At age 100, Mama still talks about her childhood in great detail, and remembers with remarkable clarity what happened 80 or 90 years ago. As we worked in the Shop just the other morning, Mama started talking about her youth... and got on a roll:

> *Oh, I had the greatest of childhood fun. I had big pigtails as well as big feet! There were ten of us children... seven boys and three girls. Never a lonely moment. Papa was a good provider and family man. Papa was a farmer. We had cows, hogs, chickens, dogs, and cats. We never went to bed hungry. All had plenty of food. Mama worked hard, canning berries in the summer and drying apples in the fall out on a sheet on the tin roof. I never realized how hard Mama worked until I grew up into it myself: Cooking. Cleaning. Washboard laundry. Sewing. In the winter, Papa would kill at least three hogs, and every piece of those hogs fed the family. Mama made sausage and souse... and it was so good! All ten of us had chores. Papa always kept two cows, and one of my favorite things to do was to watch my brother, Allen, milk the cows. Allen didn't like milking, so, sometimes, he'd add water to the bucket to shorten his task.*
>
> *With seven brothers, growing up could be dangerous at times. One night when our parents weren't home, my older brother, Rex, decided to explore the*

attic. It was dark up there, so he got out Papa's torch... a crude lamp that burned kerosene. Rex lit the torch as I watched him make his way up the narrow staircase. Curiosity got the better of me, and as I pushed my way past him, my hair caught fire! We scrambled to prevent my pigtails from burning and got the fire out. Rex and I had great difficulty explaining to Mama the toasted strands of hair around my face.

Breakfast was a big deal. There were twelve mouths to feed, and we all ate together. Every morning, we'd have fried meats, molasses, eggs, and wheat bread. Then there were chores... and school. We had cornbread every day. When we were in school, Mama sent us along with a biscuit for our lunch with preserves we had made ourselves. Mmm! For supper, Mama would have vegetables. In cold weather, one of my chores was to keep the wood box filled with dry wood and kindlin'. We had a big, comfortable home. No electricity and the only running water was the spring down the hill. Our heat was by the kitchen wood stove, a fireplace, and a wood stove, so keeping that wood box full seemed like a full time job when it was cold. We had a well boy, built by Uncle Bert. It was quite the modern convenience, because I don't think anybody else around here had one. It was a bucket on a large pulley wheel and a rope, which we could lower downhill out of sight to the mountain spring. (Around here, nobody had a well, either.) We learned by feel when the bucket had hit the spring by a 'thunk' on the rope. Then pulling that well boy filled with water back uphill was the hard part. No small child could do it. With no running water in the house, that was how we got our water for our large family. Anyone who's hauled buckets of water uphill can appreciate what a luxury that well boy was!

The Home House was a big old country house, with a dirt floor basement, where Mama would put up her canning and wine. On the first floor was the kitchen, dining room and living room... and a hall with Mama's organ. There was music. Upstairs were three bedrooms (Mama and Papa's room had a fireplace), and on the third floor were two beds.

Papa had two horses and a wagon—one time he had two mules—and he would trade, or barter, whatever he had to offer with others. They met up at Amherst at the mill. People would bring shares of corn for grinding into cornmeal, and they would bring an extra share to trade. That's how most people did business in those days. Or, if Mama needed to go into town to buy anything, she would have to go down to the James River, cross over by ferry to the train stop at Abert in the morning, ride seven or eight miles in to Lynchburg, do her shopping, and then take the train in the afternoon from Lynchburg out to Abert, ferry back across the River, and then home. I don't recall ever going along with Papa or Mama when they went to town... only that they were gone for a long while.

I loved to go to the Post Office. I'd catch one of our horses—Almeda, the big brown one, or Dan, the black one—by the mane, and lead them over to a fieldstone to step on so I could climb up. Then off I'd gallop... bareback, of course! When I got to the Salt

Creek Post Office, I'd hop off onto the big rock outside the door and tie Almeda or Dan to the hitching post.

When Saturdays came, we were all very happy, because we knew that on the next day, Sunday, we'd get to go to church. There was no work on Sundays. We girls never wore pants; always long dresses. We made most of our own clothes. It was a great time for us. We'd all get dressed up in our Sunday best and go with Papa to church. He was the superintendent and I played piano. Sometimes we walked a mile to church. Other times, Papa would hitch up his team and say 'OK, everybody into the wagon!' and we'd all load up. Mama would pack a big basket for lunch and we would spend all day at church. Mama said the white dresses would be just a-cracklin'. Well, we usually went on foot, and we would march down to the church. We didn't go down the road... we cut across the field. There was a swamp down there, an' your shoes would get muddy even if it won't rainin'.

At an early age, I took music lessons from Mr. Warner W. Slaughter. He taught me the rudiments of piano, and I learned to play hymns. I became pianist for the church at age 13. Playing church music is my greatest joy. I seldom missed Sunday school or worship service. I got paid three dollars a month to play the piano at church... and I played that piano for over 70 years. And you know I still love to play, whenever anybody has a request, but I've got to see the notes.

Mama deeply loved and admired her parents. Papa Henry Burton crossed over in November of 1959, and

Grandma Hattie in 1972. At age 100, Mama has seen just about everything. She lost a son to a heart attack in 1997, and her husband to cancer a year later. But the only time I've ever seen Mama cry was when her mother died.

We all have powerful memories of the Home House, just over a mile down the road from the Shop. It really was a wondrous place, brimming with music and laughter and the wonderful smells wafting from the kitchen. We were allowed to be kids, yet we learned a strong work ethic by watching and by pitching in. We learned the values of integrity and responsibility. We learned the importance of family—although I don't think we fully realized it then. We would be much poorer without those experiences, even the difficult ones. And I know that my siblings and I wouldn't be who we are without our extraordinary parents who led by example.

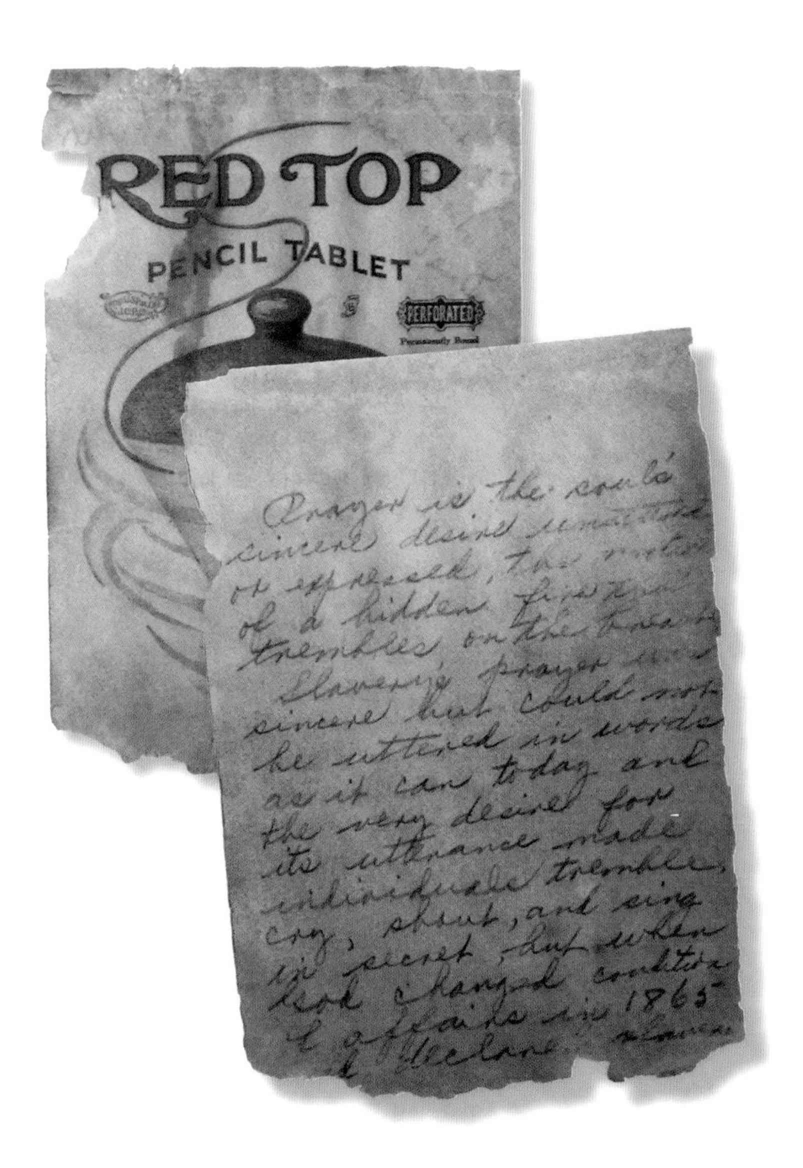

Prayer is the soul's
sincere desire unuttered
or expressed, the motion
of a hidden fire that
trembles on the breast.
Slavery's prayer was
sincere but could not
be uttered in words
as it can today and
the very desire for
its utterance made
individuals tremble,
cry, shout, and sing
in secret but when
God changed condition
of affairs in 1865
and declared slaves

Daddy and Ottie Green were cousins, both of them grandsons of Wyatt Woodruff. Ottie's wife, Martha, was the longtime church secretary and historian who prepared this speech, early 1900s.

No longer standing is the building that housed the United States Post Office at Salt Creek, Virginia (est. 1856). More often than not, mail arrived by ferry over the James River rather than by land.

Daddy's Dad: "Papa" Walter N. Woodruff (center) with his grandsons, our brothers, Walter "Doll" (L) and James "Bug" (R), circa 1945.

Mama's Dad: Our grandfather, "Papa Henry" Burton. (His son-in-law, our Dad, James E. Woodruff, is in the background on the left.)

Facing page: Mama's Mom: "Grandma Hattie" Burton, circa 1900.

1961: Grandma Hattie Burton with the Author, age 2.

Now faith

is the substance

of things hoped for,

the evidence

of things not seen.

— Hebrews 11:1

Mama and Daddy, circa 1965. Mary Fannie Burton married James Earl Woodruff on 11 May 1934. They would welcome five children between 1935 and 1959, the Author being the youngest.

chapter 2

Mama & Daddy

"Where are we going, Daddy?" I asked. (Riding in the car with Daddy without the rest of my family along made me feel special—it was just my Daddy and I.) I had been watching him carefully load boxes and brown paper bags of groceries from the store into the car when he helped me into the front seat. I strained to see over the dashboard, wondering about our destination this time. "You'll see soon enough, Angie." As Daddy turned off of Elon Road onto an unimproved dirt drive and started up the hill and into the woods, I watched him for a clue. Daddy seemed as calm as always, even a little blue, but he had a familiar twinkle in his eye.

The driveway was steep, and the bare Virginia red clay and rock had ruts so deep that Daddy had to carefully and slowly navigate. We bounced along. When we pulled around a curve and into an opening in the woods, I saw a few scrawny chickens scatter around the side of a dilapidated old house. A young girl with a dirty face peered through the screen door. Without a word, Daddy started unloading the bags and boxes onto the front porch, and a woman wearing a rumpled apron emerged, wiping her hands on a rag. She wiped her brow, maybe a tear, and shook my Daddy's hand with both of hers. As Daddy drove us back home, we didn't say a word.

Only as I grew older did I begin to understand a bit of just how much Daddy and Mama did for others in need. I'm sure I will never know the full measure. Many years after that special delivery—after I had re-opened the business, a woman approached me and said, "If it hadn't been for your father, my family would have starved to death."

With vivid memories like these, I am reminded that the upbringing my siblings and I had was an extension—a passing of the torch—of the timeless values and character instilled in our parents in a very different day and time. So let me take you back.

On the 28th day of August 1912, Walter and Aurelia Woodruff welcomed their fourth child, named James Earl, to the world. Daddy grew up on Wyatt's Corner, just as his father had before him. There was a responsibility to that—an awareness that Daddy carried with him throughout his life. And he lived it quietly every day.

When Mama—Mary Fannie—was born four years later into the Burton household just a half-mile down the road on the 24th of November 1916, it seemed predestined that these two little ones would spend their lives together. They met at a very early age, and their mothers were the best of friends. Mama recalls:

If it hadn't been

for your father,

my family would have

starved to death.

— a family in need, to the Author

Mama Hattie Burton told me that when I was just a baby in the crib—about five months old—James Earl, who was just four or so, was visiting with his mother, Aurelia Woodruff. Mama and Aurelia were the best of friends. Mama said that little James was watching me in my crib and she asked him if he wanted that little baby. He said, "Yes'm, I'd love to take her home!" About 16 years later, on May 11, 1934, James did take me home to be his wife. That beautiful marriage lasted 64 years. James was 21 and I was 17 when we were married, on a Saturday—just before Mother's Day—at the home of our pastor, Dr. James A. Shelton. James Earl's sister, Lucille, and Mrs. Delia Slaughter were present to witness our marriage. (I still have my wedding dress.) For a time, James and I lived with his father, who had become a widower about four years earlier.

In 1935, James and I became the parents of a big, ten-pound baby boy. We named him James Earl Woodruff, Jr., but his grandfather nicknamed him, 'Bug.' In 1937, our second child, Walter Allen, was born. We called him 'Doll,' because now his older brother had a doll to play with. People called him Doll all of his life. After fourteen years of wanting a baby girl, in 1951 we were blessed with twin girls, Leona Darnette and Hattie Darnelle. Then, in 1959, our baby, Angela Cheryl, was born. James was so happy with his children. He loved his family and was such a good father; he was always there for them.

Before my parents were married, they both attended the same two-room schoolhouse—Chestnut Grove Elementary—at Salt Creek. Many siblings and relatives of both Mama and Daddy attended the same school. Mama recalls the primer and the readers she used to use, and tells us that she was *"a very good student. Not extra good, but very good."* One of her standout memories, however, she recounts with a laugh; for drinking water: *"there was one bucket of water—and one dipper!—for the whole school!"*

About 1933, at age 21, Daddy joined the newly-created Civilian Conservation Corps, which provided camp-like meals and lodging (and military-like order and discipline) for young men doing the hard labor in building trails, lodges and other facilities in more than 800 parks nationwide. They upgraded many state parks, improved forest fire-fighting techniques, and built a network of maintenance buildings and public roadways in remote areas. The men were paid a small wage—about $30 a month—but were required to send at least $25 of that home to their families. It was part of President Franklin Delano Roosevelt's New Deal... under the Works Progress Administration. It was real work for a country struggling to come out of the Great Depression. Daddy's CCC camp was on out Elon Road and up on the Blue Ridge at Snowden. They were building that section of the Blue Ridge Parkway. Mama has letters that he wrote home from that CCC camp.

Daddy's experience in the CCC made him more employable, and he landed a job with a steel firm at Holcomb Rock. Mama recalls that Daddy had to walk down to the James River and row himself across it in a boat to the plant at Holcomb Rock on the Bedford County side. The walk alone each day was about five miles round trip. When that business closed, Daddy went to work for Glamorgan Pipe

& Foundry. Lynchburg was the first city in the South in which cast-iron was made, and by the 1930s, pipe and fittings had become one of its principal industries, employing some 600 workers.

While Daddy worked his factory job, Mama cared for their two young sons, our big brothers, Bug and Doll. She looked after Papa Woodruff. Mama also worked outside the home, and one of her jobs was working in the orchards nearby. The foothills of the Blue Ridge are famous for peaches and, most notably, for apples. Mama recalls:

> *At harvest time, the women put on pants and worked hard in the orchards, picking peaches and then apples. I worked in Scott's, Dawson, and High Peak orchards, filling box after box with fruit. The highest amount of money I made in one day was three dollars. Out there in the gang of pickers with me were my mother, Hattie Burton, Mrs. Martha Green, Mrs. Delia Slaughter, and Aunt Marinda Parks. One day, we went on a strike for more money. The boss, Luther Johns, came by one hot September day to find that we had turned the wooden apple crates over and everybody was sittin' on 'em. When Mr. Johns inquired as to the problem, our spokesperson, Mrs. Green, told him we wanted more money. And we got that raise! I don't even remember how much it was—ten cents maybe—but we made our point. I also worked as a housekeeper and a nanny in the David Hugh Dillard home. We referred to that house as 'the mansion.' It was so large. I took care of the baby of one of the Dillard daughters, and enjoyed working there until I became pregnant with the twins.*

He administers justice

for the fatherless

and the widow,

and loves the stranger,

giving him food and clothing.

— Deuteronomy 10:18

Our brothers were about 16 and 14 when Mama and Daddy welcomed my fraternal twin sisters, Darnette and Darnelle, into the world in 1951.

Long before we were here, our Corner—Wyatt's Corner—had been known as a good place to stop. It had been so for the weary travelers on foot, on horseback, or by cart or wagon coming down off the Blue Ridge, or about to head up into it. In Wyatt's day, he let them camp there, and Wyatt's Corner and his hospitality became known far and wide. Later, when the Lynchburg transit company was sending a lone bus out on Elon Road, our Corner was known as "Wyatt's Stop." And when school buses started to run, ours was the obvious corner. Papa Woodruff watched the children loading in the morning and unloading from the buses in the afternoon, and had firmly suggested countless times that the kids needed a shelter from the elements, and that Daddy was the one to build it.

Brother Bug recalls that for quite some time, Elon Road (State Route 130) was under construction. Seems it had been since 1933. It is a beautiful road, a designated scenic Virginia Byway, that winds nearly 35 miles from US 29 in Madison Heights to US 11 at Natural Bridge. The state road workers often parked their huge rock crusher on our Corner. But once Daddy decided to build in 1951, he told them they'd have to find someplace else to put it.

And when Daddy set his mind to something, everyone knew it would be done well. He dispensed with Papa Woodruff's great idea for a bus shelter for school children, and started planning something much grander. Daddy handed the keys to his truck to Bug (then 16), and started sending him down to Campbell Avenue in Lynchburg for load after load of cinderblocks. Bug says he loaded every cinderblock in that building by himself and by hand. Although it was hard work, we don't think Bug minded getting to drive at all. Daddy had a friend over in Madison Heights who was in the construction business, and he assembled a crew. Small mountains of gravel and sand came and went. There were stacks of two-by-fours and piles of re-bar and hammers were swinging. They mixed mortar with a wheelbarrow and a shovel. Even at age 73, Papa Woodruff kept the shovel moving to keep the mortar from setting up. Because there was no running water at the Corner, they had to go through the woods across Elon Road to a spring, and haul water back by hand in buckets.

All of the men pitched in for the building, and when they broke for lunch, Mama and Grandma Hattie kept them fueled with good meals including their famous fried chicken. No one seems to remember exactly how long the building process took. (Mama was a half-mile away at the Home House and was expecting twins, so she didn't get out much.) As work continued, those driving up and down Elon Road began to see a building rising on Wyatt's Corner. Passers-by sometimes stopped to watch the spectacle. *"Whatcha buildin', James?"* was a common question early on. I can just picture our proud grandfather, Papa Woodruff, explaining the finer points of construction to anyone who would listen. He knew a little something about everything.

When the dust settled in 1951, there stood a no-frills, gleaming-white, two-story cinderblock structure. Daddy beamed as Papa Woodruff winked at him. When they fetched Mama and handed her the keys to the Store with living quarters above, Mama was pleased as well. Her mind was set on making it a home first and then outfitting a well-stocked cash grocery and filling station.

Mama and Daddy, and Bug and Doll, and twin baby girls moved into the upstairs of the building and made it their home. (They still had no indoor plumbing and there was an outhouse out back.) Even before they opened the store, Mama and Daddy had started taking in foster kids. Among the first was Shirley, who Mama said was such a sweet, nice girl... and a lot of help around when the twins were born. Mama had her hands full, and they soon set about to stocking and opening a cash grocery, which for many years would be one of the only stores around.

Daddy worked most of his adult life at the foundry, retiring at age 62 in 1974. By that time, Mama was a veteran shopkeeper; she had been running the Store for 22 years. Daddy didn't care much for being idle or confined to the Store, so he spent most of his retirement days farming. Mama remembers:

> *James always wanted to fix broken things himself; he insisted on saving every possible penny. He did not like to make too many bills. (When he died, he didn't owe anyone.) And a fixer he was! But James could be real careless at times, and he was teased quite a bit about his farming mishaps. He turned the tractor over more than once. He had a freak accident with one of his trucks and broke a toe, which put him in the hospital for eight days. He chose to do his own plumbing, electrical, mechanical work. We'd all get very nervous when he began to pull out his tools.*

Once, after repairing a leaky roof, James started down the ladder face out. Sure enough, after a few steps, the ladder began to careen forward, landing James on his face and splitting his lip among other things. Another time, James and my brother, Melvin, had gone out to work on the cattle fence. Now, Melvin was big, and loud, and often wore a shirt that said, 'Here Comes Trouble.' Well, one day, James and Melvin had the tractor out with an auger attachment to drill post holes. They were gone for awhile and next thing I know, there's Melvin standin' at the back door in nothin' but shirttails and boots, holding his leather cowboy hat where his pants used to be! Seems he got too close to that auger while it was spinning, and it ripped the pants right off o' him! He said to my husband, 'James, you're tryin' to ruin me!' For a long time, those shredded pants hung on the barbed wire fence to mark the spot.

James was a loving, kind, gentle soul. He couldn't say 'no' to anyone. His children and grandchildren adored James and were always following him around.

Our Daddy had a favorite poem that he read and talked about often. It summed up his philosophy. It was how he lived his life.

The House by the Side of the Road

There are hermit souls that live withdrawn
In the peace of their self-content;
There are souls, like stars, that dwell apart,
In a fellowless firmament;
There are pioneer souls that blaze their paths
Where highways never ran—
But let me live by the side of the road
And be a friend to man.

Let me live in a house by the side of the road,
Where the race of men go by—
The men who are good and the men who are bad,
As good and as bad as I.
I would not sit in the scorner's seat,
Or hurl the cynic's ban—
Let me live in a house by the side of the road
And be a friend to man.

I see from my house by the side of the road,
By the side of the highway of life,
The men who press with the ardor of hope,
The men who are faint with the strife.
But I turn not away from their smiles nor their tears,
Both parts of an infinite plan—
Let me live in my house by the side of the road
And be a friend to man.

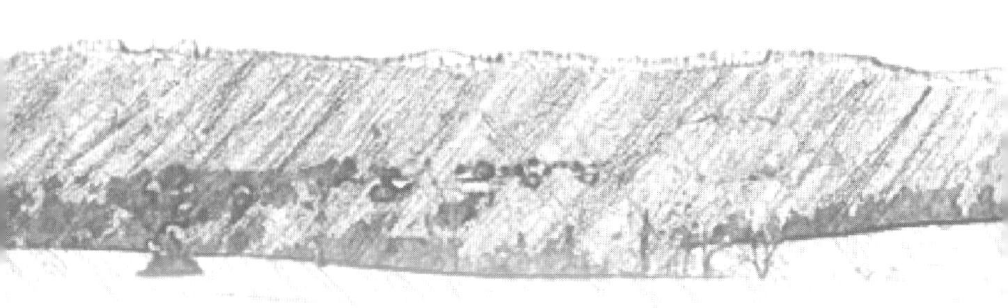

I know there are brook-gladdened meadows ahead
  And mountains of wearisome height;
That the road passes on through the long afternoon
  And stretches away to the night.
But still I rejoice when the travelers rejoice,
  And weep with the strangers that moan,
Nor live in my house by the side of the road
  Like a man who dwells alone.

Let me live in my house by the side of the road—
  It's here the race of men go by.
They are good, they are bad, they are weak, they are strong,
  Wise, foolish—so am I.
Then why should I sit in the scorner's seat
  Or hurl the cynic's ban?
Let me live in my house by the side of the road
  And be a friend to man.

— Sam Walter Foss

(June 19, 1858 — February 26, 1911)

1—Alice Woodruff
2—Mary Fannie Burton
3—James E. Woodruff
4—Marian Leftwich
5—William Leftwich
6—Harry Rucker
7—Bertram Woodruff
8—Harry Snead

Chestnut Grove Elementary, the two-room schoolhouse at Salt Creek, Virginia. circa 1928

Above: Our future Daddy, a young James Earl Woodruff, about age 21. Circa 1933. Civilian Conservation Corps, Camp F-10, Co. 354. Snowden, Virginia.

Above: Mama and Daddy on their Wedding Day: 11 May 1934.

Left: Mama and Daddy pose for an engagement photo, 1934.

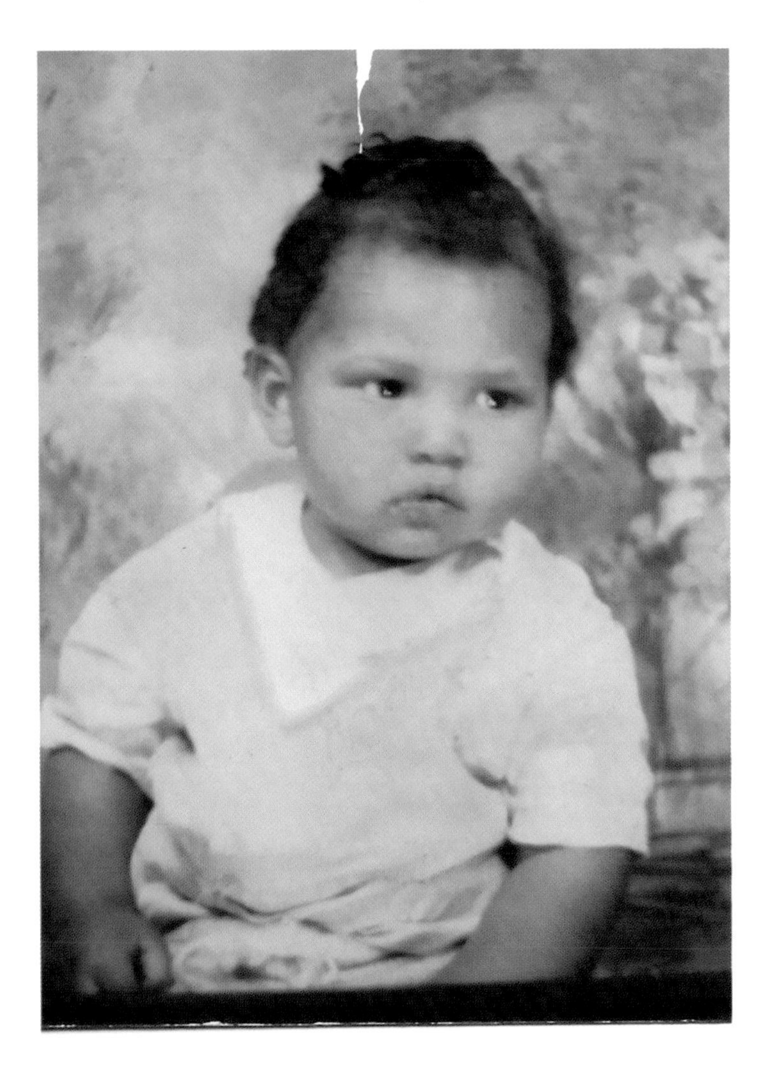

The elder of our two big brothers, James E. Woodruff, Jr. (better known as "Bug," so named by Papa Woodruff). Bug was born in 1935, 24 years before the Author.

1943: Our brothers, Walter "Doll" (left) (1937–1997), and James Jr. "Bug" (b. 1935).

Mary Fannie Woodruff—Proprietor—1952.

chapter 3

Mama the Proprietor

"Lord, have *mercy!* Everyone ok?" shouted Mama at the sound of a gun shot. Except that the shot rang out not from a gun, but from inside the cast iron wood stove, nearly blowing the lid off, and causing the stovepipe to come crashing down, sprinkling the floor with soot. *"Oh! My!"* she exclaimed as she caught her breath. *"Must've been a bullet in the stove! Land sakes, we've got to be more careful what we put in there. Thank God nobody was hurt!"*

Mama remembered this gem just the other day:

> *Well, with so many customers comin' and goin' all the time, naturally they tracked in a lot of stuff. Seems like we were always sweeping up, and we got into the habit of dumping whatever was in the dustpan into the wood stove. I reckon one of our many hunters was fishin' in his pocket for cash and dropped a round of ammo on the floor. Or maybe I dropped it—we sold a lot of ammo, you know, all kinds. Nobody saw the bullet in the dustpan when we swept up, and so it*

went into the wood stove, which was always burnin' in the cold months... it was our only heat. And then, POW! We laugh now, but what a scare we all had!

Usually, things were a bit more peaceful. But my sisters and I had a good laugh again when Mama asked Darnette to help her pull the bag out of the vacuum cleaner. As Darnette was completing the task, Mama said, *"Put it in the barrel,"* (meaning the trash burning barrel). Then, Mama quickly said, *"No, on second thought... better not burn it, 'cause it might have a bullet in it!"*

Papa Walter, whose vision it was to build something on this Corner, and who had helped—physically and financially—to bring this building into existence, was downright pleased to preside over Mama's Store every day.

"I'll have the usual," said Papa Walter as he took his customary spot. The usual was a johnnycake with cheese. The spot was an old bench beside the enormous wood stove that heated the Store. Every day, at precisely 11:30 a.m., Walter would place his lunch order with Mama, grab the day's newspaper and read it front to back, interrupted only by the occasional customer. *"Have you heard the news?"* Walter would offer in greeting, *"They just made Elizabeth the Queen of England,"* or *"that von Braun guy says they're gonna put a man on the moon... imagine that!"* or *"Harry Truman just nationalized all the steel mills!"* Walter loved to greet customers, but Mama recalls that he liked to stir up some controversial conversations, and he would hold tight to his newspaper all day long. He was always up to date on everything that went on around the world, as Mama tells it. After enjoying his johnnycake with

cheese, Walter insisted on pulling out his change purse and paying five cents for the cake and ten for the cheese. *"He always paid for his lunch,"* said Mama. Walter also kept a checkerboard nearby, always ready to challenge anyone who was up for a game or two.

Mama and Daddy had opened with $1,000 borrowed from the bank—nearly $9,000 in today's dollars—outfitting and stocking the Store. The long sign over the doorway that read, "J.E. Woodruff Cash Grocery," was punctuated at either end with Coca-Cola buttons. In addition to the mainstay of gasoline from the two pumps out front, Mama sold cigarettes. Mama hates cigarettes, but customers demanded them. Inside, there were also fresh meats, cheese rounds, bottled soft drinks, cookies, candy, bread, canned goods, coffee, milk, salted fish, flour, sugar, corn meal, large rolls of bologna sliced to order, hog feed, and ice cream. In this part of Virginia, hog feed and ice cream were required inventory. With infant twin girls in tow, the work for Mama and Daddy was just beginning. In 1952, Woodruff's Store was open for business. Mama tells us more:

> *We lived upstairs, above the Store, which made it convenient for night travelers who had run out of gas or couldn't find their way. James would often get out of bed to help somebody. He couldn't say 'no' to anyone. He often delivered groceries and, later on, the girls would tag along with their Daddy.*
>
> *We had so many friends and customers who would come in, sometimes just to chat. The Store became the gathering place. There was Ottie Green, Uncle*

> *Tom Parks, Whimple Davis, Mrs. Fears, Billy McConnell, Archie Dawson and his family, the Rucker brothers from Claspie Hollow: Gene, George, Richard, Harry, the Ford brothers, Swanson Stinnette, oh, and Mittie and Haywood Duff and their children. The Humphries, Bill and Faye Dawson, and the Robert Oliver families were some of our first customers. Our little business grew, and it was a happy time.*

Mama's business became the center of the universe, at least for the locals in our neck of the woods. Mama was serving up simple fare, such as the johnnycakes, and 25¢ hot dogs. One day, a new face stopped in for lunch. He looked a bit out of place in his business suit and clipboard in hand as he enjoyed a chili dog, served with a smile. When the man asked Mama if she had a license to sell the food, she replied no, that she didn't realize that she needed one. The man nodded and smiled and suggested that she get one as soon as possible. She got one.

At some point, the Store also became the obvious choice to become a game checking station for the Virginia Department of Game and Inland Fisheries. Hunters would not only stop by to warm up by the stove or a hot cup of coffee, they could now check in their bag of white-tailed deer, wild turkey and black bear.

Woodruff's Store had become the meeting place. True to Walter's vision, it was where the schoolchildren met their school bus in the morning and unloaded every afternoon. It was where locals and travelers alike could gas up their vehicles, grab a bite, or catch up on the news. It was the precursor to the modern convenience store, but

Mama has the light

of the LORD on her face…

that is what draws people…

not so much the food,

but the comforting atmosphere.

They just love to sit with her,

and she always loves

to pray for anyone.

— the Author

with something far more important: a feeling—no—an attitude, really.

A curious thing began to happen. Mama and her customers realized that the Store was a place of nourishment. A safe haven. A place of refuge. A place where people felt welcome and comfortable, regardless of race or nationality. Mama encountered all sorts of situations: folks needing a phone, women escaping abusive husbands, hungry folks without the ability to pay, hunters with a chill seeking a warm wood stove and a hearty meal, schoolchildren waiting for their bus or for their parents to pick them up, and those hurting who just needed a friendly smile and a place to be. Mama was always glad to help them in some way. She has a special gift of making folks feel comfortable, welcome, and cared for.

In the early years, Mama had some regular customers who were standouts for various reasons:

MR. CHARLIE was a warm and friendly local handyman of Monacan tribe heritage. He worked for Daddy for a number of years, helping with the farm—chickens, hogs, and cattle.

MRS. MITTIE DUFF lived about half a mile away, and walked to the Store to get groceries for her family. She was also of Monacan descent. Often, she would sit and rest for a while by the wood stove, and talk with Mama about life. Any time that Mrs. Duff was there enjoying some of Mama's food—a johnnycake was the usual—she would say, "This is *delicious* good." It stuck.

Mr. Henry Robinson stopped in daily for an ice cold bottle of cola, into which he would dump peanuts, and then turn the bottle up and swig it down without stopping.

There was another man with a great big heart and a drinking problem. He could sing and play the guitar. Mama and Daddy became his audience, listening to his songs as well as his stories of hopelessness. At times, his wife came running from his drinking to the Store.

Mr. and Mrs. Oliver were our neighbors... almost like family. She played our piano at the back of the Store beautifully. There were Saturdays when the Olivers would pick me up—just me—and take me over to the city for some window shopping on a stroll down Main Street. The fact that they were white and I was black never occurred to us.

Old Mr. Cabell lived nearby in a house with no electricity or running water. He had no family of his own, and so on a regular basis he would ride his horse over to the Store to be a part of ours. When Mr. Cabell could no longer take care of himself, Mama and Daddy took him in and cared for him until he passed away.

Meanwhile, the twins, were becoming quite precocious. Darnette has a vivid memory:

> *From the time Darnelle and I were about four years old, we would go upstairs to the windows that were facing the highway to watch customers come and go at night. It was so much fun for us to secretly watch them from above. They would laugh, talk, smoke, eat and drink, and drive away without even knowing we*

At the Store, circa 1956: Daddy was very proud of his twin girls, Darnelle (left) and Darnette. One Sunday morning, Mr. Fred Dudley from Lynchburg stopped by to snap this treasure. If Daddy was in a suit, it was Sunday.

were there. They never looked up. We were like spies. Sometimes they would argue... now that was really fun to watch. There was this one short little woman who always had a cigarette dangling from her bottom lip... while she talked, while she shopped, while she loaded her car. It just dangled there. This woman always seemed to be angry with someone, and one day it was Mama's turn. Seems the woman had racked up quite a bill on her charge account at the Store, and hadn't made a payment in quite some time. When Mama gently inquired as to when she might expect to be paid, the woman became belligerent and, storming out of the store, demanded that Mama meet her out in the parking lot to settle it. At nearly twice her height, Mama chuckled to herself and said, 'Ain't no way I'm goin' outside. I got work to do.'

Mama always seemed to be able to handle any situation, including flimflammers. Darnelle and I were teens when the flimflammers came one time. It seems like such a small thing now, but it was a really big deal back then. We had heard tell of flimflammers in the area, but we were caught off guard. My first clue that something was wrong was when I heard the cash register drawer slam shut and Mama raise her voice. This meant something was terribly wrong. Mama, agitated, said, "I don't know what he wants!" I looked up and two men were leaving the store. Mama said one of the men tried to confuse her by placing a large bill on the counter then taking it back and placing a smaller one down. He tried to tell Mama she was giving him the wrong change. The second man came in the door and asked the first, "What do you want, man?" That's when Mama said, "I don't know what he wants!" Then both men left the store. We were safe. Mama had saved the day again.

As my twin sisters were growing up in the 1950s in a busy Store, Mama and Daddy figured that they were done having children of their own. After all, there were large gaps between the boys, Bug and Doll, born in 1935 and '37, and the twins, Darnette and Darnelle, 14 years later in 1951. So Mama and Daddy were taking in foster kids whenever the need arose. In 1958, Mama and Daddy discovered that they had another child on the way, and I was born in February of 1959, eight years to the month after my twins sisters. Daddy was 46 and Mama 42, and that put a span of 24 years between my oldest brother and me.

As a young girl, I didn't realize that my upbringing was preparing me for what I would face in the future. Had I known then, I might have run away. Or perhaps I would have paid more attention. All of the ups and downs of growing up in this Woodruff family would shape me—painfully at times—to carry on, no matter what.

Trust in the Lord

and do good;

Dwell in the land

and feed

on His faithfulness.

— Psalm 37:3

August 1952: Mama's brother, Uncle Rex, came down for Home-coming and the Store's grand opening in his 1950 Buick Special.

The "Coke buttons" started flanking the Woodruff's storefront sign before the Author was born.

J. E. WOODRUFF CASH GRO.

GROCERIES
AND MEATS

76 Gas & Oil
Monroe, Va., 24574
Phone 384-1708

DATE ______________________ 197__

M ______________________________

	1		

Plate A

Mama's Store doubled as a game checking station for the VDGIF. Here, she checks in a black bear taken in the mountains nearby.

April 1963: Daddy's sister, our Aunt Lucille (left), and Mama on the Corner with the Author at age 4.

Our neighbor, Mrs. May Oliver, played the piano at the back of the Store beautifully. The Olivers were like family and were particularly kind to the Author.

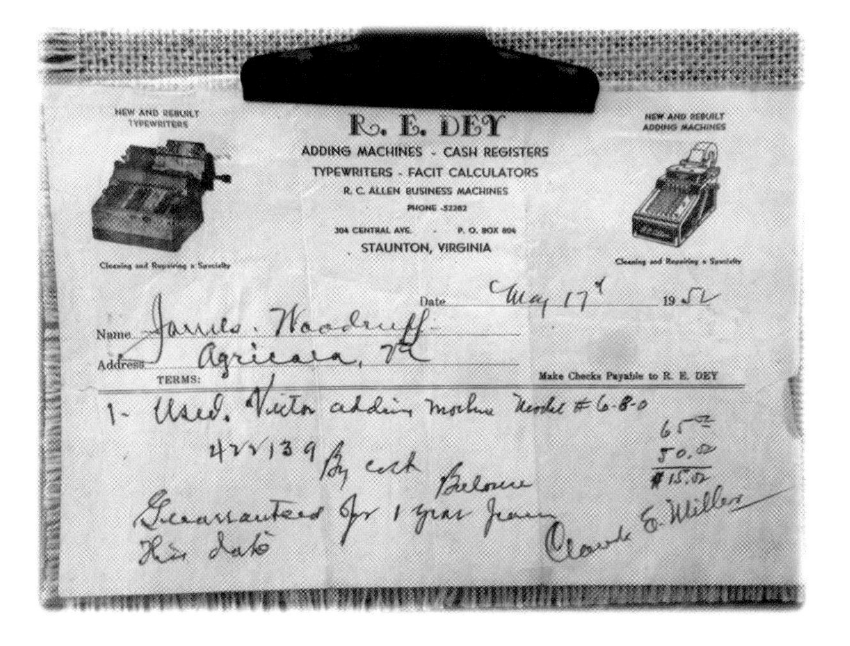

NEW AND REBUILT TYPEWRITERS

Cleaning and Repairing a Specialty

R. E. DEY

ADDING MACHINES - CASH REGISTERS

TYPEWRITERS - FACIT CALCULATORS

R. C. ALLEN BUSINESS MACHINES

PHONE -52282

304 CENTRAL AVE. - P. O. BOX 604

STAUNTON, VIRGINIA

NEW AND REBUILT ADDING MACHINES

Cleaning and Repairing a Specialty

Date May 17th 1952

Name James Woodruff

Address Agricola, Va

TERMS: Make Checks Payable to R. E. DEY

1- Used Victor adding machine Model #6-8-0 65.00

422139 By cash 50.00

Balance $15.00

Guaranteed for 1 year from this date

Claude E. Miller

At left: The original used adding machine from 1952 remains on display in the Store. Above: The original receipt for that adding machine, dated May 17, 1952.

The Author outside the Store at the age of 8.

J. E. WOODRUFF CASH GRO.
76. Gas & Oil

The Author on the back porch side of the Store on a Sunday in 1964.

Growing Up Woodruff

"DARNETTE, JUST WHAT COLOR were you *aiming* to get?" said Mama, looking stunned when Darnette showed up with a new hair color. Mama declares that Darnette is going to continue to do things to her hair until her head "is as bald as a baby's behind." Mama's quick wit never fails. She is part poet and part comedienne. At least she shoots straight with us, and over the years we have found that she is almost always right.

My twin sisters have eight years' head start on me, and they are often the bridge between my generation and the older ones. After all, my oldest brother and I are nearly a quarter-century apart. Both Bug and Doll had joined the Navy and I hardly knew them growing up.

My twin sisters are another story entirely. Darnette and Darnelle were born in February of 1951 after 14 years of Mama and Daddy praying to have a little girl. They were doubly blessed! On the 20th of February that year, Mama was at the Home House going into labor. As Mama tells it,

Grandma Hattie was there, and Dr. Leon Braswell was in the house. The good doctor didn't know that his name was about to be carried into the Woodruff family.

Dr. Braswell (b.1904—d.1958) had his office over on Fifth Street over in Lynchburg, and he practiced medicine from 1937 to 1958. We found out later that in 1949, he was named Virginia Vice President of the National Medical Association. Mama remembers him for his kind face, with a pencil-thin mustache and spectacles.

Twins were expected; the doctor had told Mama early in her pregnancy that he heard two heartbeats. Mama and Daddy had been praying for so many years for a little girl, and Grandma Hattie was eager to have a granddaughter named after her. The firstborn was indeed a girl! She didn't cry, and one leg was not straight. Upon seeing this, Grandma Hattie said, "No, not that one." So, after Doc Leon took the baby and broke through the ice formed on top of the basin on the back porch in order to dip her in it, she cried. Mama says, "She screamed for six weeks. She had colic." Mama insisted that this little girl would carry a variation of the doctor's name. And so Leona Darnette it was. Twenty minutes later, the second baby came into the world—also a girl—and Mama decided that she would be known as Hattie Darnelle.

Darnette is the problem solver. She is a fixer/maker, good at working with her hands. She is creative and has a certain flair. She is bubbly and energetic and when she enters a room, the party starts. Life would be boring without her. At the same time, she is a very patient person. Her experience as an MP in the Army doesn't hurt. Darnette is a breast cancer survivor—twice. Darnette is the only one who can make our fried pies to perfection, just the way Mama did, and Grandma Hattie before her.

Darnelle is the optimist. She always has a smile on her face and a good attitude. She is prayerful. She is great at bookkeeping. She is a semi-retired school teacher as well as an ordained minister of the Gospel. She exhibits many qualities of our Daddy, including having a hard time saying 'no' to anyone. Darnelle, who started working with me in the Pie Shop in 2013, is our customer service pro.

Even though we lived out in the country and our world consisted of little more than the farm, the Store, and school, we always felt loved... not from an overt show of affection or words, but from the confidence we had in our parents. We never went hungry. And although some might have thought our family to be of very modest means, we never felt poor or thought that we lacked anything. We were happy, and felt blessed.

Daddy's quiet, gentle strength made us feel safe, and we sisters would rather to have died than to disappoint him. As we were growing up and becoming more independent, he would gently, but firmly, say to us, "Girls, you've got to stand on your integrity." We understood. He never ranted or raved. Even when one of us did disappoint—and those times came—he never pointed a condemning finger. Daddy would gently lead us on and encourage us to make wiser decisions moving forward. He was our rock.

Mama's peace, strength, and wisdom have always amazed us... even to this day. Her work ethic would make the aver-

You've got to stand

on your integrity.

— James Earl Woodruff, Sr.

age person buckle. How she ran that Store, and reared five kids of her own plus the foster kids, and is joining the elite fraternity of centenarians, is beyond us. We believe that the secret to her longevity is her attitude:

> *I'm so glad I learned to trust Jesus. The Lord has truly blessed me! He has been my guide through my entire life. It pays to serve Jesus every day. My mother taught me to be a good wife and mother, and I did my best to instill this into my girls. Trusting the Lord and passing on good values pays off as one grows older. I often sit in my bedroom, night after night, thinking back through the years. I think about family members who have gone on to Glory. My thoughts run back to the simple times with loved ones: good conversation over hot cocoa or sodas, home-cooked meals, telling jokes and singing. Singing and playing instruments was our favorite thing to do. Lawn chairs and barbecues and good friends and family reunions. Being a blessing to someone in need. Kids and foster kids and grandkids and great-grandchildren.*

These are the things that matter to Mama.

Mama is also known for her razor sharp wit, and she rarely pulls any punches. My sisters and I have burned indelibly into our minds many of her witticisms, which we have found to come in handy quite often.

On the Lord's Name:
"Never, never, never say, 'OMG.'"

Thoughts on a nursing home:

"You know, if you got a good mind, and go in a place like that... you subject to lose it!"

On marriage:

"Girls, you gotta work at a marriage. That girl's parents were not a good example: she saw her father put a gun to her mother's head. That wouldn't have happened but one time for me. I'd be like a chicken topping tall corn: scratch, eat, and be long gone!

On the Kitchen fire:

"I wonder, just how much grease did Larry have in that skillet? I reckon it was just enough to make a really good fire!"

On a nearby live Nativity Scene:

"Shucks, I bet all them men are from Monroe!"

Diagnosing Mechanical Problems:

"Something in my car sounds like bees: Bzzz–bzzzz. You hear it?"

On Darnette's frequently misplacing her keys:

"Lawd, have mercy! I'll tell you right now, if you want a key lost, just give it to Darnette!"

On raising chickens:

Did I ever tell you what a chicken looks like with the cholera? When they start walking like this... and their red comb turns pale... they are surely going to DIE!"

On taking medication:

"Hattie, look at my legs. Those pills have got my legs looking like broomsticks!"

On cats:

"Those cats are so pretty. I'd like to let mine in, but I don't believe them flea collars do any good. And if you bathed him, he'd probably die!"

On truth:

"They tell me if you throw a rock into a pack of dogs, the only one that will holler is the one you hit!"

On raising hogs:

"If a hog is po, he'll be streaked with lean. That's streak-o'-lean! If he's real fat, that's where you get fatback!"

On making pies with not-quite-ripe fresh fruit:

"You got to let the sugar fall!"

On Dancing with the Stars:

"I get so tired of them naked women turnin' their legs up on this here television!"

–or–

"You know, one of them fell off the stool; he looked just like a monkey!"

On breakfast:

"I fixed me a big bowl of corn flakes with some chocolate milk... and it was some kind o' good!"

On the State of the Union Address, 2006:

"Look, there's Condoleeza Rice. She took what's-his-

name's place... you know, the man they say is kin to Bush... they say it's his cousin—Gomer Pyle."

On church potluck food:

"Lawd, that macaroni... you could bounce it like a ball... and I don't know what they did to those string beans, they tasted like somebody cooked 'em in coal oil... and the chicken, it was this here part!"

On clutter:

"Now, that child was up there tryin' to dress in that room that looks like Noah's Ark... you know, it was a mess!"

–or–

"There is everything in this room from amazing grace to a floating opportunity!"

–or–

"This room looks like the wreck of the Hesperus!"

On proper stovetop temperature:

"You don't ever need to turn nothin' up on red."

On preachers:

"That preacher is looking for somewhere to light."

–or–

"That preacher had on a red coat, white pants, and red & white shoes. He sho' didn't look like no preacher!"

On the remedy for foot pain:

"You need to go to the drug store, and get you some medicated bunion pads... and stop wearin' them stilts!"

On taking supplements:

"I've seen you take about 10 pills... you look like a chicken pluckin' up corn!"

On enunciation:

"Some man called my house this morning and I couldn't understand his name, or a single word he was sayin'. It sounded like: wickety-wack, wickety-wack, wickety-wack!"

On poor choices:

"Now that's the way people do... they go all around the rose bush, and light on a gypsum weed. Now, a gypsum weed is a stink weed."

On wise choices:

"You happy right."

On scanty attire:

"That dress was tight as Dick's hat band!"

On the company one keeps:

"Lie down with dogs, and get up with fleas."

On how to avoid catching cold:

"Y'all better come in outta that night air!"

On complications:

"It would take a Philadelphia lawyer to figure this out!"

Mama Grammar Person:

"Did you say, 'Where's it AT?' It's between the A and the T on Preposition Street."

All God's Children

"Do you want to go to school?" Mama asked the barefoot boy. Charles was about six years old. His clothes were tattered; his feet calloused and dirty. He lived about a mile away in an apple orchard with his widowed father—one of Daddy's friends. The boy was my age and frequently walked over to the Store for food or candy, but he was not attending school. Charles gazed longingly out the big storefront window at the other children boarding the school bus. *"Charles,"* Mama insisted as the bus pulled away, *"do you want to go to school, too?"* Hearing her the second time, Charles glowed, *"Yes'm, I want to go to school!" "Well, then,"* Mama said, *"you'll need some school clothes. Go home and get your things; you can stay with me, and I'll send you to school."*

Later that day, Mama found Charles standing at the front door with the tracks of tears on his cheeks and a battered old suitcase—presumably with all of his worldly belongings—in hand. Charles did go to school, and stayed with us until he was old enough to strike out on his own. Today, Charles is married and has a beautiful family. He always remembers Mama, especially at Christmastime and on Mother's Day.

The story of Charles is just one of many foster kids welcomed into our home. Families in the community knew it. The local kids knew it. Even the folks at the county social services knew well that when all else failed, they could rely on Mama and Daddy to step up when needed. Mama remembers some of the other standouts:

James and I started taking in needy kids very early on... even before we ever opened the Store. When we did open for business, our twins, Darnette and Darnelle, were infants. Before we moved into our living quarters above the Store, we were living at the Home House, and I was longing for some help. Just about then, social services called, looking for homes for a couple of teen girls. We took them both in. One of them was a handful of trouble from the start—stealing and such—and didn't fit in very well. The other girl was Shirley... such a sweet, nice girl and so much help with housework and the twins. Shirley stayed with us until she finished high school and later married a wonderful young man. They have a grown daughter now. Shirley stays in touch and never forgets me on Mother's Day and at Christmas.

Joyce was a pretty young girl who was in the foster system after being given away by her father, and needed a home. She became like a daughter to me, and a real sister to my girls, and remains so until this day.

One very cold February evening, a social worker came by to ask if we could help her out with little twin boys until a permanent place for them could be found. They were from a large family and had a number of other siblings, including another set of twins. These two boys had no shoes. They hadn't had any shoes for so long that their feet were crusted over... just awful. Those boys, Donnie and Phillip, were about four years old when they came. They loved us and called us Mom and Dad. They stayed until they were 18. They did not look like twins and were also different in every other way. Donnie was studious, quiet, and sometimes sneaky—getting out of chores whenever he could; Phillip was a good worker and loved being outside on the farm, where he helped James a lot. Phillip is still single with one son. Donnie married a lovely woman and they have beautiful twin girls who are mirror images, as well as a son named Donnie. Those boys are in their 40s now, and they bring their families to visit often.

Welcoming those in need is something we saw Mama and Daddy do time and time again. They learned it from their parents. Everyone still talks about the time that the home of Papa Henry's sister, our great-Aunt Marinda, burned entirely to the ground, displacing a family of two adults with nine kids. Papa Henry and Grandma Hattie—with 10 children of their own and without hesitation—took Marinda's entire family in for the duration.

My sisters and I have always considered it to be a privilege and a blessing from above to be a part of the Woodruff family. But life is not always a bed of roses and, to be certain, challenges lay ahead—some of them quite serious.

For I was hungry

and you gave Me food;

I was thirsty

and you gave Me drink;

I was a stranger

and you took Me in.

— Matthew 25:35

1970s: Foster son, Donnie, twin brother to Phillip. In the background is the Store with its 76 gas sign and pumps.

2010: Donnie (center) was one of many Woodruff foster children who return to the Corner to visit us.

Shirley (center), one of many Woodruff foster children; here, with her husband, Carlton, and daughter, Cheryl. Shirley was of great help to Mama when the twins were born.

2001: Charles (left of Mama), one of the Woodruff foster children, and his family. Charles wanted to go to school.

Mama and Daddy all dressed up to go somewhere.
Looks like Christmastime at the Woodruff house.

Mama loves to go fishin' on the mighty James River.

Centenarian Mama still plays the organ, the piano, the ukelele, and the guitar.

55 6 7 8 10 12 14 16

Troubling Times

"Here is a bulletin from CBS News. In Dallas, Texas, three shots were fired at President Kennedy's motorcade in downtown Dallas. The first reports say that President Kennedy has been seriously wounded by this shooting," said the somber, familiar voice of Walter Cronkite. It was November 22, 1963. A Friday afternoon.

"Did you hear that?" shouted a customer. "President Kennedy's been shot!" A hush fell over the Store.

I was four years old, and doing my best to help Mama in the Store. My sisters were 12 years old and at Elon Elementary School. They reminded me recently that when they got off the school bus that day and walked into the Store, I was sitting on the knee of our Mama, and she was crying. Nearly everyone alive on that fateful day in 1963 can tell you where he was and what he was doing when the news about John F. Kennedy broke. Everyone was in shock. As young as I was, I remember the feeling with clarity. A fear came over me that I had not known before.

The voice that had spoken such inspiring words had been silenced. For my family, our hope had been dealt a serious blow. President Kennedy said, "The heart of the question is whether all Americans are to be afforded equal rights and equal opportunities; whether we are going to treat our fellow Americans as we want to be treated." When he said things like that, we believed him. We were crushed.

Looking back now gives me a perspective that I did not have then. There was an uneasiness that was pervasive. The Cold War and the arms race were in full swing, which explains why Daddy decided to build a basement under the store—*after* the fact. That involved moving rock, and using dynamite to do it (really); we were all grateful that Daddy didn't blow the Store to smithereens. Mama saw to it that the building was properly evacuated. There was a universal fear of a nuclear attack, so that new basement space was intended as an emergency shelter, and our parents began stockpiling essentials down there... just in case.

Also in motion were the many facets of the Civil Rights movement and laws that were enacted. There was a nationwide atmosphere of unrest. We could see it and hear it and feel it. In politics. In music. In big cities and small towns. Riots were occurring across America, and not all of them were faraway places. Mama's Store was doing quite well, but we were scared. We felt safe with Mama and Daddy, but everything else around us seemed so unsettled. Woodruff children had not been taught hate. We were taught to treat everyone with kindness, without regard to pigmentation or size of bank account. To see people behave otherwise was bewildering.

Until this time, most schools in America had been segregated, and many communities wished them to remain so. School integration was the law, and forced busing was being used to achieve racial quotas. In Amherst County, Virginia, however, students of color weren't exactly standing in line to attend Elon Elementary, which had traditionally been for whites only. The black kids had their own school. Even the Monacan Tribe had its own school, for they were neither black nor white. And around here, many people liked segregation, and wanted it to stay that way.

In 1963, when it came time for Darnette and Darnelle to enter the sixth grade, they were twelve years old. All of the kids—white and black—rode the same bus; stopping first at Elon to drop off the white kids before continuing on to the school for blacks. This first day of school in the fall of 1963, Mama put her twins on the bus as she always had. The difference now was that my sisters would be getting off the bus with the white kids at Elon Elementary. Papa Woodruff was confident: "We're going to be the example," he said. My sisters were the only black kids who showed up for school, and the first thing they saw when they got off the bus was graffiti spray painted on the brick wall of the school: "Go home, ________!" Darnette and Darnelle stayed. They endured the name-calling. One day, a classmate threw ink all over Darnelle's white dress. If the teacher left the classroom, milk cartons and other objects were thrown in the direction of my sisters' heads. When they were old enough for proms and other social events, they weren't welcome. Even more curious, my sisters were ostracized from the black school events as well, because they were attending the white school. They were accused of "tryin' to be white." On the school bus, others turned their backs. Although my sisters did not fully understand what was happening, they realized that the kids were parroting what they had heard around the dinner table at home, such as, "That darn old Civil Rights Bill."

When prom night arrived, Darnette and Darnelle both had dates. They got all dressed up in their best formals and had beautiful corsages. When they arrived at Central High School (the black school) and approached the table of the ticket takers, my sisters and their dates were denied entry. A group of their peers were locked arm in arm. "No, you're not coming in," they said. It happened more than once. The Ring Dance was a similar occasion.

Because they had chosen to be pioneers at the white school, Darnette and Darnelle also missed out on the extra-curricular opportunities they might have had if they had gone to the black school. They both maintain to this day that the experiences made them stronger.

(Things didn't change overnight, either: eight years later, when it was my turn to go to Elon Elementary, I was still the only black kid in the entire school. I remember feeling lonely; only one schoolmate, a white girl, was willing to be my friend. And a very good, and brave, friend she was.)

Mama's Store was a bustling business, and she had quite a number of regular customers, faces she saw every day. But now that she had the audacity to send her girls to what had been the white school, many of them stopped doing business with Mama. Then one day, a brick came crashing through one of the big storefront windows, shattering more than the glass. It really affected my self-esteem, and I was sometimes overcome with fear, and began to withdraw.

With a succession of events including the drowning of a

dear cousin of ours, and the murders of Dr. Martin Luther King, Jr. and Bobby Kennedy just two months apart, we began to wonder when it would all end. Mama remained steadfast, and reminded us that we were put on our Corner for a reason. She made certain that everyone who came to our Store felt welcome, regardless of race or nationality. In the midst of all this upheaval, Mama was having to take on even more responsibility:

There were many days, I remember, when I just wanted to close down the Store. Those thoughts came when my parents were growing old, and I felt that they wanted me to spend more time with them. Days would come and pass, and I would not have time to visit; I was always so busy at the Store. I was so glad when my sister, Othella, and her husband, Haywood, moved back from Norfolk, and took care of our Mama and Papa until they died.

Papa Henry died in November of 1959. James and I took in Papa Walter when he became disabled, and took care of him until he died in 1968. Then we took care of Mr. Ottie Cabell for a year or two before he died. James saw to his final affairs and a proper burial. Then Mama Hattie died in August of 1972. Days were sad for me, but the Store helped me keep my mind off the sadness somewhat. When James retired from the foundry in 1974 at age 62, we still didn't travel much, even though we wanted to; we both felt like we didn't have time for it. There were very few vacations for us. We did take a trip out West, to California, to visit relatives, including cousin Wiley Burton and his wife, Nancy Wilson... yes, the legendary jazz singer, and they came to visit us here, too. James and I had a lovely trip to Florida one time. But after he retired, James kept runnin' his farm and I had managed the Store... for 30 years.

As time went on, Mama found it more and more difficult to keep the Store profitable and competitive. All the new, modern convenience stores and supermarkets were putting many of the old mom-and-pop stores out of business. And so in 1982, Mama, going on 66, and Daddy, 70, made the difficult decision to close down Woodruff's Store. Many of their loyal customers begged and pleaded with them to stay open, and they did re-open for a short while before closing it down for good.

For Mama and Daddy—for the community, really—it was a sad farewell to an old friend, an institution, a way of life, for faithful shopkeeper and loyal customer alike.

Then he said to them,

"Go your way, eat the fat,

drink the sweet, and send portions

to those for whom nothing is prepared;

for this day is holy to our Lord.

Do not sorrow,

for the joy of the LORD

is your strength."

— Nehemiah 8:10

ELON
E PERCH RD

Cobwebs in the Cash Drawer

"I HAD THAT DREAM AGAIN, ANGIE" Mama said to me. "You know, the one about...." Nodding, I interrupted to finish her sentence, "I know, Mama... cobwebs in your cash drawer." Mama had always been a stickler with money, and could account for every cent. She also has dreams, and we have learned to pay attention; often they carry meaning.

So when Mama kept talking about a recurring dream of cobwebs in her cash drawer, it became clear to me that it wasn't so much about a lack of funds, but that something inside was gnawing away at her. "She's too old to run a store," I thought. But something was tugging at my heart, too: a crazy dream that I thought best kept to myself, at least for the time being.

Contrary to what some might think, life on the Corner after the Store closed in 1982 was anything but dull. The building our Daddy had built 30 years earlier took on another role: that of a place to stay for those in need. It was a great place for foster kids, relatives, others needing care...

especially once the bathroom and shower were installed on the main floor.

Our foster brothers, Donnie and Phillip, lived there for a while. Daddy had a couple of older cousins who needed a place to stay: Claudia and Kemper. Claudia suffered with extreme dementia, so her younger sister, Kemper, looked after her. During this time, Kemper was diagnosed with cancer, suffered a stroke, and died suddenly in 1988. Mama and Daddy stepped in and cared for Claudia until she, too, passed away.

Not long after that, Mama's youngest brother, (nearly 15 years younger) Luke, came to stay in our store-turned-apartment. Uncle Luke seemed to have a hard time with life, and it was good for him to be near family. Luke passed away in 2002 and was laid to rest in the old churchyard. It was a blessing to us to see the old Store being put to good use, rather than sitting there on the Corner empty and forlorn. That would have haunted us.

That Echo in My Head

All of these changes had me thinking—deep thoughts, most of which I kept to myself. So much of the life we had known was different now.

Our brothers had been married for some time: Bug married Georgianna Diggs, and they started giving us nieces and a nephew: Lillie, Lydell, and Jacqueline. (Bug's wife, Georgianna, passed away in 1990.) Doll had married Evelyn Hancock, and they had one daughter, Dana.

Of the sisters, Darnelle was the first to marry in May of 1969 to Fred Haskins, Jr. Darnelle and Fred welcomed two children, Christopher and Latanya. (Fred was killed in an automobile accident on May of 1980. He was just 34 years old.) In April 1996, Darnelle married again to Edward Winston. In 1976, Darnette married Andy Hill, and they have two children, Andrew III and Raven. In 1985, I married Larry Scott, an accomplished musician.

The old Store, and the people who frequented it, had been so intertwined in all of our lives for so long that it was difficult to avoid talking about it. Mama kept saying that she was having that recurring dream of "cobwebs in my cash drawer," and started giving voice to a longing to see the old place opened for business again.

Dare I tell her?

I was waiting tables. Tough work. I really didn't mind it much, though, because I love people, and providing good service to folks is my calling. I had been harboring a secret dream of opening an upscale café of sorts in the old Store building. That echo bouncing around in my head was unclear: it sounded like the voices of those who had gone before me on this Corner... but all talking at once, and over each other. It was almost like a gentle nagging that wouldn't let me go. I did my best to ignore it.

About 1993, we started planning a Woodruff family reunion, and set about to tracking down all of the relatives scattered around the country. The effort was monumental with many contributors, and two years in the making. Because our arm of the Woodruff family was living in the heart of family history, I rallied Mama and Daddy, my sisters, and Darnelle's daughter Latanya, and we marched off to gather all of the family history we could find. We spent hours at the Amherst County Courthouse, the Amherst County Historical Museum, and the Jones Memorial Library in Lynchburg, poring over records and books. Some of what we discovered was confirming and some was enlightening. As any family historian knows, one question answered prompts a dozen more. It never ends. But we cobbled together a nice little package of notes and made copies for those who attended a very successful Woodruff Family Reunion on July 8, 1995 at the Holiday Inn South in Lynchburg, Virginia. The joy we all felt at that reunion intensified that echo in my head. I was inspired.

Still, doubt pestered me: "You don't know anything about running a business." "You don't have the money." "You're out in the middle of nowhere." But one day in 1997, when Mama again mentioned her recurring dream, I had to spill the beans. "Mama, I want to re-open the store." Her response surprised me. She was thrilled, "Oh, boy! This is the answer to my dreams!" She smiled and nodded, "I've been wondering when you'd come around. We've got a dirty store and lots of cobwebs, but I will help you!"

My husband's reaction wasn't nearly as encouraging. "Are you crazy? You *are* crazy!" he said. "It's out in the middle of nowhere! You won't run the store, it will run you! Angie, you know you are not going to have a life any more. I don't know anything about that kind of business. I won't be able to help you."

Undaunted, I proceeded with the dream, even without a master plan. The Lord gave me a nudge. I didn't know

That was one of the reasons

I wanted to open this place:

to carry on that legacy.

— the Author

what I was going to sell. I just knew I was supposed to open it... and as time went on, I knew what I was supposed to do. It was about this time that Daddy wasn't feeling well at all. Mama recalls:

My husband James had been complaining with shortness of breath and a little pain in his chest. He was under the care of Dr. James Rodman. James had made an appointment with Dr. Rodman on July 24, 1997. As we were preparing to go to the doctor, we received a call from a neighbor of our son, Doll. 'Come to the hospital... Walter has had a fall.' Doll had suffered a massive heart attack. He died instantly. That same afternoon, James was diagnosed with small cell lung cancer. Over the next several days, we made plans for Doll's funeral service, and managed to have James keep his appointment with the oncologist. I felt our family chain had been broken. It is pretty hard to lose a child. Doll and his wife, Evelyn, would have celebrated their wedding anniversary that same week.

Doll was a happy child. He had a beautiful voice, and he loved to sing and play the bass guitar. He was dedicated to his family and siblings. He was a great father. Doll's funeral service was beautiful. There were many friends who called and encouraged us. Pastor Moore gave an inspiring eulogy, and soon we were able to turn our attention to James and his cancer treatments. James did well with those treatments. Dr. William Headley and his staff were so kind and gentle. James had good and not-so-good days, but he never complained. He was able to stay home without ever having to spend any time at the hospital.

As we mourned the loss of our brother, and Daddy's cancer treatments continued as he declined, we knew that we had to press on. By early 1998, I was in the old Store, preparing to open up my little upscale café. There was so much to be done and I was pretty much going it alone. Mama was caring for Daddy, my sisters had full-time jobs and most people were skeptical. Mama was very encouraging, but there was only so much she could do. She was 82 now and she was Daddy's caregiver, but she helped when she could and did more than I ever expected. In the mean time, I borrowed $10,000 from the bank (it was not enough), and did with it what I could.

On August 10, 1998, the old Woodruff's storefront was open for business for the first time in 16 years. If I'd had a clue as to what I was in for, I might never have done it. The early days were slow; I separated the days into two categories: "Slow," and "Dead Slow." (In fact, the first 15 years were slow.) By this time, Daddy was really sick, and on Wednesday the 2nd of September, he passed away... just five days after his 86th birthday. I remember not having but one or two customers that day. Mama remembers:

> *James passed away with his family at his side. Evelyn, Doll's wife, was there, as well as Joyce, one of our former foster children. Darnelle delivered the eulogy the following Sunday. We said good-bye to our wonderful husband, father, and friend.*

When I opened in '98, I really had no idea what the future held. I knew that I had been given this vision by the Lord, but I really had no direction as to how to proceed. I didn't say, "OK, I'm going to open up a Pie Shop and make lots of money." I simply had a vision that I was supposed to re-open the family business and that was it.

For years, things at the Shop were going so wrong for so long, that I kept asking the Lord why He wanted me to re-open this Shop in the first place. I wasn't making any money... couldn't even pay myself. I worked long hours and put so much effort into it, and still, customers were very hard to come by. As we went into the autumn that year, I remember trying so hard to draw customers to the Shop. Really hard. I tried so many different things and still there was no business. Mama remained ever-faithful: "You gotta have faith, Angie; it's gonna be OK," she would say. "Now faith is the substance of things hoped for, the evidence of things not seen." That passage, Hebrews 11:1, was always there in my mind. Sometimes I couldn't hear it, but it was there. I think that's what kept me going for quite some time. But I didn't even know it. That faith—that resilience to make things work and just to keep trying no matter what. That kept me going. Faith has a lot to do with this whole thing. Mama's faith. She knew it was going to be good. She knew that it was going to be OK... sooner or later.

As time went on, things at the Shop remained painfully slow. I had to borrow money from the bank to stay afloat, (not good business practice, I know), and my husband and I were becoming more and more distant, because he had told me not to open the place, and I did it anyway. He didn't like to see me struggle. Things were really tough, and I often daydreamed about having a nice car and a nice house. Every day, I'd look out the storefront window and watch the cars passing by. I was discouraged.

Things at the Shop

were going so wrong

for so long,

that I kept asking the Lord

why He wanted me

to open this place.

— the Author

Along the way, I got to know a gentleman by the name of Earl Stinson. He was a Navy veteran of the Second World War. He was one of the founders of Hunters for the Hungry. He was successful in business, and invested in the community. He owned a meat packing plant—Green Valley—among other business ventures, including an ostrich farm. Mr. Stinson got into the habit of going around the area and re-opening old country stores that were boarded up... more because he held a belief that they *should* be open, rather than making him a lot of money. As we got to talking, he offered to buy my business, rent the building from me, and oversee operations, with me running it day to day. I hated the thought of selling it, but I was relieved to have help, so I accepted. Immediately, Mr. Stinson plowed cash and other resources in to the Shop; he brought in a soft-serve ice cream machine, ostrich eggs and those pastel-colored eggs from Araucana chickens, grocery items and other novelties, including bait. He showed me the ropes. After a couple of years, when he and I felt that I was ready to take the helm, he made it very easy for me to buy everything back from him. Mr. Stinson passed away in March of 2010. I will always be grateful to him.

Then one autumn day, a young woman walked in and said that she needed a job. I had no intention of hiring anyone; I wasn't even able to pay myself at that point. When she walked in, she looked forlorn, worn... tired. Life had beaten her down; she and her young son had been living out of her car. She really did need a job. I learned that her name was Angela, that she was from California, and discovered that I liked her. I didn't know exactly why at the moment, but I did. So I promised that "AJ" could have a job and stay on until winter, when I knew that what little business we had would drop off to dead slow. Wintertime is really tough; but even though things were really slow, I was able to make ends meet, and AJ did well. As her time at the Shop was about to come to a close, she found a job, had some help from folks at her church, and landed squarely on her feet. She is now married—sister Darnelle officiated—and AJ remains a good friend of the family to this day.

As I learned what worked with customers and what didn't, it was clear that desserts were far outselling any of the deli items. So I decided that I was going to focus on pie. Why? "Everybody likes pie," I reasoned. The only problem was that now I would have to learn how to make a really good pie. Mama has always been a wonderful cook. She mastered the fried pie and the sweet potato pie. But she was so busy with everything when I was growing up that I never really learned to cook the way I wanted to. I learned much from my mother-in-law, who has a special talent and a special coconut custard recipe. I also learned from Mama's sister, Othella, better known to us as "Aunt Putt," and from the *Southern Living* cookbook she gave me. That book has turned out to be one of the best gifts I have ever received.

My pie work has involved a lot of trial and error, and a lot of guessing. Sisters Darnette and Darnelle tease me in good fun about burning pies. I tend to be a perfectionist, and sometimes a pie just doesn't turn out. After thousands of pies, I've learned a few things. I've learned that a good fruit pie has to bubble. I have learned the little nuances that I use to adjust on-the-fly in the kitchen, such as when the peaches aren't quite ripe or are less than fully flavored. I must be getting the hang of it, because an interesting thing happened a few years ago. I call it a God thing. And it helped in part to change the course of the Pie Shop.

Back in the fall of 2012, it was pretty much business as usual. The leaves in the foothills of these Blue Ridge Mountains were just beginning to put on their annual show of color. That's a spectacle that people travel from all over the world to see. As usual, Mama was seated in her customary spot, having opened the Shop that morning, peeled apples for pies, and chopped celery for the chicken salad to be made that day. Then a new face walked through the door. She was young, and pretty, and lost... seeking directions to an orchard nearby.

When I asked if she would like a cup of coffee or a slice of pie, her eyes lit up, and she sat down to one of our tables. She introduced herself as Stephanie Granada, a writer for *Southern Living* magazine. She was traveling through rural Virginia for an article on the apple harvest. She was very sweet, and seemed to really enjoy the slice of warm apple pie I had served. As we gave her directions to get back on the road and headed in the right direction, she snapped a few photos, we said good-bye, and I didn't think much more about it... until the September 2013 issue of *Southern Living* hit the streets. Inside this issue entitled "The Sweet Taste of Fall" and with a beautiful pie on the cover, there on page 70 was a little, and I mean *little*, blurb in fine print mentioning Woodruff's Café & Pie Shop, with these words:

"Stop for the best apple pie ever (yes, really ever)."

"That's it?" I thought. It wasn't until people from all over started showing up at the Shop with their copy of the magazine in hand, that I realized that those words had an echo, they were resonating, and the tide had turned.

Over the years, we have had some nice coverage—from little write-ups to feature articles—in various publications, including the *Richmond Times-Dispatch*, the *Roanoke Times*, the Lynchburg *News & Advance*, the *Amherst New Era-Progress*, the *Staunton News Leader*, *Lynchburg Living* magazine, and *Ageless Woman* magazine. But nothing holds a candle to that one little blurb in *Southern Living*.

When 2014 rolled around, going on 16 years in business, things had finally turned the corner. The very best advertising—word of mouth—was kicking in. Oh, we hadn't "arrived" by any means, but we were seeing a change for the better that looked as if it were going to stick around. As word continued to spread, we found our circle to be ever-widening. We have had customers from interesting places all over the world. We've had people embark on a 3- or 4-hour drive just to experience Woodruff's, stay for awhile... and turn around and make their way home. Another customer came in recently from about 90 miles away to sample some pie and to tell us that our story had inspired him to start a soup kitchen in Charlottesville. Things like that just bless our hearts!

In March of 2014, we were recognized by the Virginia General Assembly with House Joint Resolution Number 467, with Delegate Ben Cline and Senator Tom Garrett as the patrons leading the charge:

2014 SESSION • Virginia General Assembly

14105386D

HOUSE JOINT RESOLUTION NO. 467

Offered March 3, 2014

Commending Woodruff's Café and Pie Shop.

~~~

Patrons—Cline and Garrett; Senator: Garrett

~~~

WHEREAS, Woodruff's Café and Pie Shop, a family-owned and -operated business in Monroe, has provided hospitality to the community for over half a century; and

WHEREAS, originally built by James Woodruff as a shelter for local school children to escape the elements as they waited for bus transportation, the building transformed into Woodruff's General Store in 1952; and

WHEREAS, the Woodruff's General Store became synonymous with hospitality, as James and Mary Woodruff would provide food for families and individuals in need, regardless of their ability to pay; and

WHEREAS, in 1998, Angela Scott, daughter of James and Mary Woodruff, opened Woodruff's Café and Pie Shop where the General Store once stood; and

WHEREAS, as a small business, Woodruff's Café and Pie Shop supports the community by buying locally grown produce from Morris Orchard; and

WHEREAS, in September 2013, Woodruff's Café and Pie Shop's apple pie received the honor of being labeled the "best pie ever" by Southern Living Magazine; and

WHEREAS, with the help of Angela Scott's mother and sisters, Woodruff's Café and Pie Shop remains a family business; Darnelle Winston handles invoices and bookkeeping, Darnette Hill makes the shop's bestselling apple pie, Angela Scott is the head cook and proprietor, and Mary Woodruff continues to have a steady presence at the shop, sharing family stories and lively conversation with guests; and

WHEREAS, over the last 16 years, Woodruff's Café and Pie Shop has continued the family tradition of caring for one's neighbors by not only providing good food and great conversation, but also supporting local businesses and the citizens of Monroe; now, therefore, be it

RESOLVED by the House of Delegates, the Senate concurring, That the General Assembly hereby commend Woodruff's Café and Pie Shop; and, be it

RESOLVED FURTHER, That the Clerk of the House of Delegates prepare a copy of this resolution for presentation to Angela Scott, proprietor of Woodruff's Café and Pie Shop, as an expression of the General Assembly's respect and admiration for the family's commitment to providing both quality products and hospitality to the members of the Monroe community.

ઌ

What an honor!

We have also been featured on local television and Bob Grebe did a nice segment on our Pie Shop for his series, *Bob Grebe's Virginia*. But the video that takes the pie was recorded early in 2015 when Rick Seback and his crew from WQED Pittsburgh came down to the heart of Virginia to spend a day with us. Rick and his crew were cris-crossing America in search of really good pie, and he found us! Rick is an energetic, jovial guy and something of a celebrity, but he remains very down to earth. What a long, fun day that was! We ended up in a segment of Rick's PBS show, *"A Few Good Pie Places,"* which first aired in August of 2015, and has been rebroadcast numerous times since. It is even available on DVD.

Recently, Sweet Briar College, the historic women's college just up the road near Amherst, has been ordering pies in quantity. Just this week, they ordered twenty and we delivered, thinking that they'd be in good shape for awhile. The next day, they ordered ten more, which were delivered at 4:00 p.m. Two hours later, they called to say that they were out again!

After so many years of business drought, it is a blessing beyond measure to know that what we do here at the Pie Shop is warmly and enthusiastically received.

In March of 2015, Rick Sebak and crew came down from WQED-Pittsburgh for a visit. We were featured in a segment of his PBS video, *"A Few Good Pie Places,"* which first aired in August of 2015 and has re-aired numerous times since.

The Lord gave me a nudge.

I didn't know what

I was going to sell.

I just knew I was

supposed to open it...

and as time went on,

I knew what I was supposed to do.

— the Author

In the summer of 1998, the old storefront may not have looked like much, but a whole lot of preparation was going on inside.

Grand Re-opening Day: August 10, 1998.

Open for business.

But those who wait on the LORD

Shall renew their strength:

They shall mount up

with wings like eagles,

They shall run and not be weary,

They shall walk and not faint.

— Isaiah 40:31

When I opened in 1998, I sold convenience store items alongside a small deli. Here, around Christmastime, Darnette, and Darnelle's daughter, Latanya, visit with Mama.

All in the family: Twin sisters, Darnette and Darnelle, Mama, the Author, and Darnette's daugher, Raven.

(dappled) light on the region

TAKE THE LONG WA

Jump on the **Blue Ridge Parkway.** (Milepost 76.5 is a great photo op.) In Monroe, stop for the best apple pie ever (yes, really ever) at **Woodruff's Cafe & Pie Shop** (4) (434/384-1650; closed Sunday and Monday), family owned since the 1950s.

HAVE A SIP

Cider roots run dee these parts. Visit pl

Above: The first customers as a direct result of the September 2013 issue of *Southern Living*.

Facing page: On page 70 of the September 2013 issue of *Southern Living* magazine, Stephanie Granada wrote a little blurb about the Pie Shop. Numerous visitors have come from many miles away with a copy of this magazine in hand.

Pie is home.

— the Author

Learn to do good;

Seek justice,

Rebuke the oppressor;

Defend the fatherless,

Plead for the widow.

— Isaiah 1:17

James Earl Woodruff, Sr. (28 Aug 1912—2 Sep 1998). Daddy crossed over five days after his 86th birthday, and less than a month after we re-opened the Shop.

Twin sister Darnette is the master of the Fried Pie, far and away our most popular item. Her technique has been handed down through Mama and her mother, Grandma Hattie.

At Woodruff's,

we love our customers,

and they know it.

— the Author

If you sell

somebody something,

make sure you give 'em

a full measure.

— Mary Fannie Woodruff

Twin sister Darnelle is our customer service pro, and also knows her way around the kitchen.

FRESH BAKED
PIES
SERVED DAILY

chapter 7

The Usual Suspects

"Mr. Couch is here, Mama! Oh, *my*! Who's he got with him in the car?" Mr. Couch was a kind, gentle widower who had become a good friend to us all, but especially to Mama. He was lonely, and he came to the Shop frequently to sit with Mama and talk. They comforted each other, and always enjoyed each other's company.

This particular day when Mr. Couch drove up to the Shop, there was indeed someone riding along with him. She was dressed all in black. We couldn't see her face, but there was an impressive hairdo. We glanced at each other excitedly, eager to meet this mystery woman. He hadn't breathed a word about this to us.

When he entered the Shop by himself, our tension mounted. Why didn't he bring her in? He sat down to the table with Mama as always, and they had a nice, uneventful chat over whatever it was they ordered. I can't even remember what they ordered. The only thing my sisters and I could think of was discovering the identity of this mystery companion. The suspense was killing us! Pretending to be working, we listened for the slightest clue. Nothing.

After what seemed like an eternity, Mr. Couch wrapped up the conversation, said "until next time" to each of us, and walked out the door to his car and climbed in. His companion turned to greet him. Was she pretty? How old was she? We couldn't stand it any longer. Darnette was the first one to the storefront picture window, with Darnelle and me right behind her. With palms and noses pressed to the glass, we strained as he pulled away to see who it might be. When she turned so that we could see her face, we discovered that it was a large, beautifully-groomed, black standard poodle! We're still laughing about that one.

At Woodruff's, we love our customers, and they know it. Many of those who become regulars are given nicknames... terms of endearment to help us differentiate. Some are still with us, and some are gone now, but they live on in our hearts. We love serving our customers. But as you will see, many of them have served us, strengthened us, encouraged us to keep on keeping on.

Jim Piggott, a retired pathologist, stops by quite regularly. He makes a cameo appearance in Rick Sebak's PBS special, *"A Few Good Pie Places."*

Pastor Robert Breeden, who just recently crossed over into glory, was an inspiration to us all. He was Mama's best friend. He had served in the US Army and the Marine Corps, and was a retired pastor living on the other side of the mountain in Buena Vista. Before his wife passed away from Alzheimer's, he had been her caregiver. Now he came into the Shop two or three times a week. He came up with nicknames for my sisters and me: he called Darnette and Darnelle "Joyce and Re-Joyce," and he called me "Angel." He called Mama "Mother Mary" or "Queen Mary." Mama recalls Pastor Breeden sweetly:

> *There never was a visit when he didn't have a handful of inspiration of some kind. Plants, flowers, candy, cards, doughnuts... whatnots of all sorts have graced Woodruff's ever since he started coming by. He was there to pray, to give advice, to lift us spiritually, and to just be a friend. Neither silver nor gold could ever match what Pastor Breeden has given to me.*

One day, Pastor Breeden's son pulled up to the Shop in a truck loaded with supplies. He said, "Have you ever heard of a 'pounding'? Well, you're about to get one: a pound o' this and a pound o' that. Here we go!" And he proceeded to unload huge bags of sugar, flour, baking soda, beans... the list goes on and on. What a blessing!

John Alford, is a retired attorney who has a cabin nearby. He and his lovely wife, Bettie, and their family, have been a constant reminder of what true friendship really is. John grew up around here, and remembers visiting Mama's Store in his younger days. His wry sense of humor keeps us in stitches; he's a jokester. John will occasionally give us some sage advice, but more than anything else, he loves to sing hymns with us. John has one of those Johnny Cash/Gospel-type voices and he can really belt it out. He has helped us in our second career as the Woodruff Singers. Any odd time that John comes in, we'll all gather close to harmonize on 'Love Lifted Me.' Some years back, we all sang together for a benefit at a local church, and we've been singing together ever since.

John is accustomed to sometimes heading for the piano at the back of the Shop for a round of song. Depending on what might be happening in the back, sometimes we have to stop him and say, "Don't go back there just now." The flour might be flying or one of us might be changing. John was also good friends with Pastor Breeden, and he loved to poke fun at the pastor.

Richard Zechini is a retired orthodontist who also has a cabin nearby. Mama says, "He doesn't *look* like a doctor." He is one of the Pie Shop's early customers. He is an expert woodworker and sometimes sells his handiwork in our Shop. He crafted a beautiful picnic table and made a gift of it to us for the Shop. He is always willing to help us get things done... runs to the dump, repairs, whatever. Sometimes he shows up with lunch for all of us—a refreshing change. As his surname indicates, he is of Italian heritage and is quite the Italian chef. So when we decided to do a fundraiser for a local shelter for unwed mothers, Richard helped us have our first "Italian Day" at the Shop—a big success. Richard is also responsible for Darnette's new hobby of raising rabbits.

Little Sara McCormick was born in 1998, the same year I opened the Shop. She and her mom, Liz, who makes such beautiful jewelry, come by to see us often. It has been a delight to watch Sara grow from infancy into a fine young lady; now, she's almost as tall as her mom.

There was the late Charles Winfree; his nephew, Donald Hendricks, and the guys from Community Funeral Home stop by to say 'hello' and we all talk about the good ol' days.

Then there are the Nixons who give us an update on their latest project. It's always good to see Greg, Christine, Catherine, the Fergusons, and the Kings—Anne and Ronnie—stop by often.

NELLIE is a lovely person who comes in every day for coffee, and is always bringing us something... bags of ice, for example. She is very kind.

THE DAWSON BROTHERS are farmers who grew up nearby and our families have always been close. Grandma Hattie was their housekeeper and nanny back in the '40s. Their niece, Pam, is close, too. When my sisters and I were young, the races were quite separate, but you never found a hint of separation between the Dawsons and the Woodruffs. The Dawson boys often bring us some of their bountiful harvest.

DAN THE "PIE MAN" is a true prayer partner, standing in the gap; he is one who walks the talk. He is known in wider circles than ours for his quiet generosity. As for the Pie Shop, he brings us new customers, he buys pies—sometimes buying us out at the end of the day— and gives them away as a ministry. And he serves as a Field Tester in our Quality Control Department. Dan is truly a blessing. Plus, he is good friends with...

Steve the "Pie Boy." Steve found us one day in 2005 as he was riding his motorcycle toward the Blue Ridge Parkway. He rode right on past the Shop, but turned around, having spied the sign touting our Fresh Peach Shakes. Steve has become like family... like a brother to my sisters and me, and like a grandson to Mama. Steve has also become our de facto PR man and storyteller backup if Mama gets tired. Steve adopted us and we him. He prays for us. While Pie Man Dan buys whole pies, Steve buys by the slice, albeit two and four slices at a time. He makes a cameo appearance in our segment of Rick Sebak's PBS show, *"A Few Good Pie Places."* If you watch closely, you can see Steve enjoying a slice of pie at a table with Mama.

Bill Hurt is a regular who loves good homemeade soup and likes his iced tea with very little ice. Bill and Mama love discussing current events.

The Dream Home Team. One winter some years back now, business was "dead slow." A construction crew was working on a cabin about a mile away from the Shop, and these guys would come in every day for a hot lunch and a place to warm up. We started cooking special meals for them that weren't on the usual menu, such as fried chicken. They gobbled everything up as we got to know them better each day. One day, Mama was expressing concern about our leaky roof, and how we couldn't afford to do anything about it. They said they'd take a look. Before long, they were back in force with tools and ladders and shingles. We had a new roof—no charge.

The Golden Girls

During my early years open, we had the pleasure of meeting a few nice ladies who were up in age; they loved meeting, eating, and chatting at the Shop. We called them the "Golden Girls." They were all single ladies, all with a story of life to tell—each different, but somehow the same.

LAVENIA — was very special to all of us. She had to use a walker to get around. She used to come to the Shop and sit all day with Mama, often with a pair of knitting needles in her hands, yet worrying that she was "in the way." The Pie Shop was her home. One cold, wintry day, we noticed that she was coughing. As she left the Shop, she assured us that she was going to get a prescription filled and would see us the next day. When she got to her house, she fell outside, unable to get up, and died. One of our comforting thoughts through this tragedy is that her last day in this life was a beautiful one at the Shop with people who loved her. She was at home with us. Mama still speaks fondly of Lavenia.

BEVERLY – first stopped in one day after seeing our sign out front for "Fresh Fruit Milkshakes." Beverly's family is from Pennsylvania. She moved here with her husband a few years back, but he has since passed away. She loves to come in and tell stories of her six children. She always seems to know just what a kitchen needs. She has often come in bearing useful gifts: mixers, aprons, the list goes on. Beverly had a son, Mike, who later moved down to live with her. One day she poured in the door crying. Mike had gotten stung by a yellowjacket while cutting the grass, had an allergic reaction, and was rushed to the hospital, where he passed away. Leaving the hospital in shock, Beverly didn't go to her house; her first stop was to see us at Woodruff's.

Catherine – would come in every other day to talk and enjoy a hotdog. She loved gardening. One day, when she fell out front, my husband and my brother-in-law rushed to help her. They were just picking her up when a truck stopped, and a guy jumped out and asked my husband what he was doing to the old lady!

Edith – had daughters I knew from school. She was always up to date on all the health news. Whenever Edith headed toward the Shop, she would always stop at the health food store on the way and bring us goodies.

Norma – is our cousin, and the one who first coined the nickname, the Golden Girls, when she would come in and see these ladies sitting with Mama. She is a family historian and a talker. Norma always has something to say and expects everyone to listen.

Leah – is a retired school teacher. In fact, she was one of my teachers, in the eighth grade. She and her husband, a dermatologist in Lynchburg, lived nearby and they stopped occasionally. He died suddenly while duck hunting in December, 2000. She came by often after that and would talk to Mama. Those visits provided a good dose of comfort food, with the accent on comfort. Leah very much wanted the business to succeed, and she has done what she could to promote it. Over the years, Leah has sent many people to us. Sometimes she picks up a few items for us if she is going to the store and we need supplies. If she's a member of our designated "Golden Girls," then she's Dorothy—tall, with a deep voice, and a little "edge" in her perspectives.

There are many other regulars who have earned nicknames. Often, it is Mama who confers the titles. The nicknames are terms of endearment to help us distinguish between our loyal customers as we talk about them daily. There is "Ponytail," of course "Pie Man" and "Pie Boy," and more recently, "Book Man."

One good friend who comes to mind again and again is chef Candace, who tracked us down at the Pie Shop in 2013. They were new in town then and after she tasted a slice of our apple pie at "Market at Main" in Lynchburg, Candace brought her husband and young son to the Shop, and she ended up rolling up her sleeves as an employee, helping with our menu, peeling apples, whatever needed to be done. They found a family away from home. Candace and her husband, Greg, helped us with our website. Their young son calls me "Aunt Angie." To me, Candace is the little sister or daughter I never had.

After all these years, I have learned that it's people who matter most. Take care of that, and everything else falls into place.

Bear one another's burdens,

and so fulfill

the law of Christ.

— Galatians 6:2

Facing page: Pastor Robert Breeden was a true friend to us all, but he was Mama's best friend.

When pie is consumed

for research purposes,

it contains no calories.

— the Author

Facing page: "Pie Man" Dan and "Pie Boy" Steve congratulate each other on their excellent taste in pie.

Above: Ronnie King (left) and Cecil Powell with Mama.

Neal and Faye Massie with Mama. Neal put up all of our signs, and helped us to open the Shop.

The Dawson Brothers: Buddy (left) and Harry.

John Alford, the man who keeps us laughing and singing.

Above: "Golden Girl" Beverly and her son, Mike. Our kitchen would not be as well-equipped as it is without Beverly.

Cousin Norma with Mama. Norma is the regular who coined the term, "Golden Girls." Norma always has something to say.

Edith (left) and Lavenia—two of the "Golden Girls."
Regular Bill Hurt is in the background.

Regulars: Standing (L to R): Pastor Robert Breeden, Leah, John, and the Author. Seated: Mama, Jim, and Bettie.

Richard Zechini.

You prepare a table before me

in the presence of my enemies;

You anoint my head with oil;

My cup runs over.

— Psalm 23:5

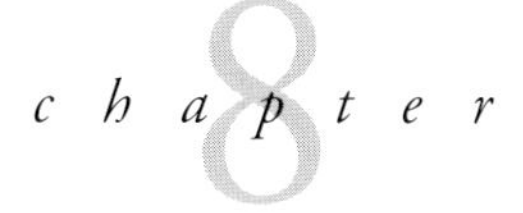

Homecoming

FOR AS LONG AS ANYONE CAN REMEMBER, including Mama, there has been Homecoming. We know that it goes at least as far back as our great-grandfathers on both sides of the family. It is an unspoken tradition—an expectation—dating to the earliest days of our home church, Chestnut Grove Baptist. The church devotes the entire third Sunday in August each year to the Homecomers, far-flung aunts and uncles and cousins and friends who come from every corner of America to Wyatt's Corner. On the day before, Woodruffs and Burtons and related kin converge on the Pie Shop expectantly. It is always the first place they stop. When August rolls around each year, my sisters and I know that we'll need to really ramp up pie production.

The third weekend in August is usually the height of peach season in these foothills of the Blue Ridge. We make the most of it with peach pies and fresh peach shakes, and it conjures up childhood memories of enormous peach cobblers, which to us seemed to be as big as the kitchen table. Each year, Mama and Grandma Hattie, and later

Aunt Putt, would prepare weeks ahead for Homecoming. As relatives poured in, the place was calm chaos. They brought with them campers and tents, cots and sleeping bags and lawn chairs; they filled the Home House inside and out. Everyone pitched in over an abundance of food, as joyful relations caught up on all of the family news since last year. There were usually new babies in their mother's arms, children running and squealing and playing hide-and-seek, just as my sisters and I did long ago. The hot, humid summer days near the James River were greeted by laughter ringing up with the smoke from barbecue grills. At twilight we caught fireflies in the glow of the bonfire, and stayed up giggling way past bedtime as the grown-ups talked late into the night. As the occasional June bug buzzed on the screen of the open window, we would drift off to sleep, feeling tired, full, and loved. These are the scents and sounds of a family institution colorfully embedded in our memories. This August, 2016, Homecoming did not disappoint; it is wonderful and reassuring to see friendly, familiar faces, and meet new ones. As time goes on, the recollections are often bittersweet as we miss those who have crossed over. We talk about Wyatt, Papa Woodruff, Papa Henry and Grandma Hattie, Daddy, brother Doll, Fred, Aunt Putt—so many others. We talk about what a reunion, what a celebration it's going to be when we see them again in glory. Mama gets both teasing and respect for reaching her 100th year. When Monday rolls around, we all wonder where the time went as we say our farewells: "See y'all next year!" echoes across the churchyard. Homecoming remains a very special time each year; and so the tradition continues.

"Come on, girls," cries Mama, ringing her little tea bell, "we've got a request." Because we often sing for our customers (now that people have seen it on TV, there can be an expectation), Mama has a signal to gather us together from our various corners of the Shop to sing a special request. When we hear the tea bell, we know it's time to sing. And so we gather, wiping our hands on a kitchen towel or brushing the flour from an apron front, putting a stray wisp of hair back into place, and sing in harmony. Sometimes it's a birthday or anniversary. Other times, we'll sing a favorite: *"I'll Search Heaven for You."* We love singing together, and as I listen to our voices in harmony, I am reminded of how very blessed I am.

We've got Mama joining the exclusive ranks of centenarians. I've got Mama and my big sisters working side-by-side with me every day. We get to make people smile. And we are honoring the legacy that was handed down to us. This is what echoed in my head so many years ago. This is what I dreamed. Even though there is so much work involved, it is truly a joy to behold what has become of that nudging I felt every time I looked at that old building. I am relieved that I never succumbed to the nagging temptation to give up. Woodruff's Café & Pie Shop is alive and well.

These days, there are no ordinary days. It is very gratifying to see our customer base growing dynamically; every day we come in to the Shop, eager to see what God has in store for us. Even at age 100, Mama is still the first one in the Shop every morning... early. The Shop opens at 10 a.m., so as my sisters and I trickle in, Mama has already peeled apples for the day and chopped celery for the chicken salad. We quickly catch up on any news as Mama takes her special chair at her usual table. Shortly before opening time, Mama calls us together for devotion. She'll read Scripture and we pray together hand in hand—every day. Then she'll say, "Flip the Open sign!" and we're ready for another busy day. Mama presides over the front of the Shop greeting customers and being the "entertainer," as she calls it. Darnette takes her place at the station for making her fried pies, our best seller. Darnelle is usually at the register and handling the phones and other front-end operations, while I head back to the kitchen to make pies. We are blessed with some faithful employees who have fully embraced the Pie Shop and everything it is. They, too, help to make it special.

In telling our story, I have been looking back in amazement at what the Lord has done. I see laughter and really happy times. I see a whole lot of hard work... a *whole* lot of hard work; only God knows what has been required of me these last 18 years. There has been some heartache thrown in, too. I see the struggles that God used to mold and make me over the years. I can see now what He was doing all along, even though it made little sense to me at the time.

Back then, I had no idea what was in store, but I see now that faith yields results and perseverance through trials pays off. We still have struggles every day, but we have seen the Lord remain true to His Word. And He has blessed us with so many friends who have helped us along the way. Some of them have gone on now and are sorely missed. Yet it seems that every day we meet new faces who come to share this special place, this hallowed ground, this little Shop on a country corner where our family stretches back for many generations. Yes, they come for the pie, the fried pies, the seasonal shakes. But those who return again and again come for something less tangible but far more meaningful—it's an atmosphere, that comfort, that feeling of being at Woodruff's. It is difficult to describe. It is greater than the sum of its parts.

Mama regularly quotes and paraphrases Scripture. One we often hear is found in the sixth chapter of Luke, just after the Beatitudes, verse 38. Jesus said:

> *Give, and it will be given to you: good measure, pressed down, shaken together, and running over will be put into your bosom. For with the same measure that you use, it will be measured back to you.*

I like to think that our ancestors, those who paved the way—great-grandpa Wyatt, Papa Woodruff, Papa Henry and Grandma Hattie, Daddy, and others—are smiling upon us as they see what this special place has become, the little things that happen just about every day on the Corner.

Above and Facing: Mama leads us in devotion each morning before we open the Shop.

Below: When Mama rings the tea bell, we sisters gather to sing.

Epilogue

"THE NEW OVEN SURE IS MAKING A LOT OF NOISE," said Mama, as I walked into the Shop and set down my purse and car keys. 'Oh, no... *now* what?' I thought to myself, hearing a noise from the oven that I knew was not good. I had come in earlier than usual, because I knew it was going to be a very busy day: we needed to fill a record number of orders. Saturdays are very busy around here. We had just remodeled the kitchen to keep up with demand: two brand new wall ovens, more cabinet space, a large island—the works. The upgrade was right on time, because the summer of 2016 was our busiest season ever.

We tripled our baking capacity, and sometimes we can produce 70-100 pies per day. As a result, even a new oven gets dirty. Fruit pies, especially, tend to bubble over. So, the night before, I had cleaned the oven.

"What's wrong with the oven?" I cried as I rushed back to the kitchen. Darnelle already had the owner's manual out and was reading it furiously. "This certainly is strange," puzzled Darnelle, without looking up. "The warranty is saying that the only way it would not be covered is if there were an 'act of God.' It doesn't say 'act of Nature.' Isn't that something!"

"I need that oven today... right now," I urged. I wasn't panicked. I was fairly calm, and I don't know why, because this day was turning out to be one of our busiest ever, and my baking capacity was severely diminished. Darnelle continued reading, "Funny, it mentions the Sabbath."

Just then, a friend of ours came in to the kitchen to say hello. Somehow, he always seems to show up just when we need him. He is a minister. "Maybe there's something I can do," he said, as Darnelle handed the manual to him. While all of this was going on, we were listening to Christian music, 'having church,' which we do sometimes back in the kitchen.

Each of us, in turn, had tried fiddling with the controls to see if we could get the oven working. Nothing. Over the rattling of the oven, our friend started speaking of a gentleman he knew who is an appliance expert. He might be able to help us. As the phone call was being placed, Darnelle walked out to the front of the store, and right into the appliance expert about whom we had just been speaking. He was enjoying a slice of our pie.

He came back to the kitchen, took one look, hit a button and, voilá, the oven started working. This is just one more of many miracle days.

This year, 2016, has been a banner year in many ways. It has been a record year for the Shop. We have made many new friends. Although we work very hard and end the day exhausted, it is a good kind of tired, rather than a weariness. I'd rather have too much to do than the alternative. There is much satisfaction in doing things well and receiving confirmation from happy customers... in seeing strangers become regulars, and friends become family.

This is also Mama's 100th year, and we are eagerly planning a celebration. We are all very excited to see this book in print and to be able to share our story with others. It is my hope that our story will be a blessing to you. An encouragement. A reason to have hope.

For although we do not know what the future holds, we know for certain who holds it. The victory is already won.

So if you live nearby, or are traveling through our special part of Virginia, my sisters, our Mama, and I hope that you will stop in to say hello, take a load off your feet and stay awhile. Now that you know us, we'd love to serve up a warm slice of pie and get to know you, too.

Let me live in my house
by the side of the road—

It's here the race of men go by.

They are good, they are bad,
they are weak, they are strong,

Wise, foolish—so am I.

Then why should I sit
in the scorner's seat

Or hurl the cynic's ban?

Let me live in my house
by the side of the road

And be a friend to man.

WOODRUFF'S
Coca-Cola
STORE
Pies
Shaker
OPEN

WOODRUFF'S
Coca-Cola
STORE
OPEN
WELCOME

Snapshots

FOR MY SISTERS AND ME, having to pore through old photos has been a good thing. Like anyone, we found old shots we had forgotten, and they prompted a flood of memories and the associated smiles, tears, and laughter. Showing these old shots to Mama has been a delight, because they often start her to storytelling of long ago. In fact, we found that Mama keeps her own stash of keepsakes in her "filing cabinet" under the red and white checkered tablecloth at her throne.

Following are some additional family snapshots of significance that I thought worth sharing. They help to visually round out our story.

The Author and her husband, Larry Scott.

At age 100, Mama still loves to play the piano for guests. Mama started playing piano at church at age 13, and was paid three dollars per month—for more than 70 years.

Mama (left) with her sister, Othella.

Sister Darnelle enjoys a laugh with big brother Walter, better known as "Doll." Doll passed away in 1997 at age 60.

L to R: Brother Doll, his wife, Evelyn, Darnette, Darnelle, and the Author.

The Pie Shop Ladies, 2012. (L to R): Darnelle, Mama, the Author, and Darnette.

Christmas 1956: Mama's Dad, "Papa" Henry Burton (age 80) with his youngest half-brother, Danas Burton (age 33). Papa Henry passed away in 1959, and Danas in 1984.

Left: Our sister Darnelle and her family in 1996. L to R: Darnelle, Latanya, Ed, and Chris.

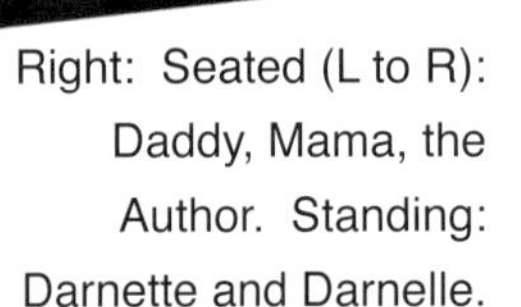

Right: Seated (L to R): Daddy, Mama, the Author. Standing: Darnette and Darnelle.

Mama & Daddy were honored at the NAACP Banquet in 1995.

Above: Our home church, Chestnut Grove Baptist, just down the road from the Pie Shop, held an Appreciation Service for Daddy. My twin sisters, Darnelle and Darnette are seated behind Mama.

Left: 1964. Mama is ready for church, songbook in hand.

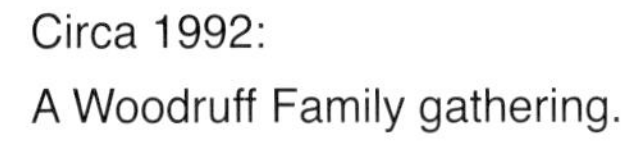

Circa 1992:
A Woodruff Family gathering.

Daddy & Mama with all five of their kids in one photo! Sisters, Darnette, the Author, and Darnelle, with brothers, James Jr., ("Bug"), and Walter ("Doll").

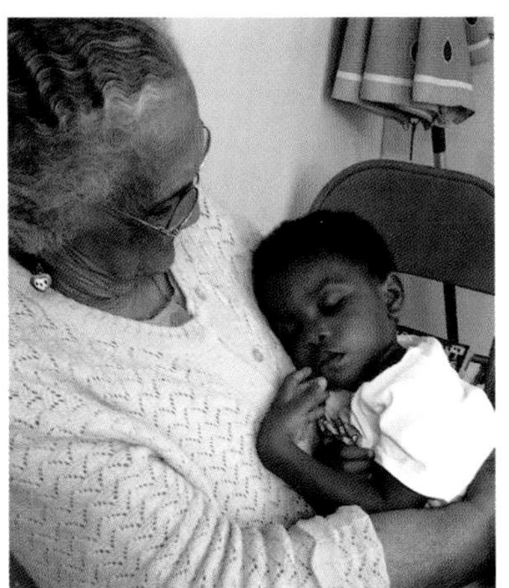

Left: Great-grandchildren are among Mama's joys.

1974: My sister Darnette joined the US Army and was an MP at Vint Hill Farms Station near Warrenton, Virginia. The VHFS was closed in 1997.

1985: The Author dances with her Daddy on her wedding day.

Darnette married Andy Hill in June of 1976.

Mama's favorite hobby is fishing.

1984: Mama and Daddy celebrated their 50th wedding anniversary.

We siblings: the Author, Darnelle, and Darnette, with our oldest big brother, James Jr. (better known as "Bug").

Milestones

1912 — August. James Earl Woodruff is born.

1916 — November. Mary Fannie Burton is born.

1933 — James Earl Woodruff joins the CCC.

1934 — May. James and Mary Fannie are married.

1935 — April. James Earl, Jr. "Bug" Woodruff is born.

1937 — January. Walter Allen "Doll" Woodruff is born.

1951 — February. The twins, Darnette and Darnelle, are born. Construction begins on the Store.

1952 — J. E. Woodruff Cash Grocery opens for business.

1959 — February. Angela Cheryl Woodruff is born.
November. Papa Henry Burton dies, age 82.

1963 — September. Darnette and Darnelle Woodruff are the first ever black students at Elon Elementary.
November. President J. F. Kennedy is murdered.

1968 — January. Papa Walter N. Woodruff dies, age 84.

1969 — Darnelle Woodruff marries Fred Haskins, Jr.

1971 — September. Eight years after her sisters, Angela Woodruff is the only black student at Elon Elem.

1972 — Grandma Hattie Burton dies, age 90.

1976 — Darnette Woodruff marries Andy Hill.

1980 — Darnelle's husband, Fred, dies in an automobile accident at age 34.

1982 — J. E. Woodruff Cash Grocery closes its doors.

1985 — Angela Woodruff marries Larry Scott.

1996 — April. Darnelle marries Edward Winston.

1997 — Walter Allen "Doll" Woodruff suffers a massive heart attack and dies, age 60. That same day, James Earl Woodruff is diagnosed with cancer.

1998 — August. Angela Scott re-opens Woodruff's.
September. James Earl Woodruff dies at 86.

2013 — September. Woodruff's Café & Pie Shop is credited in *Southern Living* magazine for 'the best apple pie ever (yes, really ever).'

2014 — March. Woodruff's Café & Pie Shop is recognized by the Virginia General Assembly.

2015 — August. Woodruff's Café & Pie Shop is featured in Rick Sebak's PBS Special, "*A Few Good Pie Places.*"

2016 — November. Mary Fannie Woodruff turns 100.

...

FRESH BAKED
PIES
SERVED DAILY

Mama Woodruff's Sweet Potato Pie

HERE IS MAMA'S COVETED RECIPE. In observance of her 100th birthday in 2016, it's her gift to you. *Enjoy!*

3 to 4 hand-size Sweet Potatoes
4 Eggs
2 cups Sugar
1 can Evaporated Milk
1 stick and a half Butter — melted
2 tsps Vanilla Extract
2 tsps Lemon Extract
1 tsp ground Nutmeg
Dash of Salt

Boil or bake sweet potatoes then mash.
Beat eggs then add to other ingredients.
Mix well.
Pour into 2 ten-inch pie shells.
Bake at 350 degrees F. for 50 to 60 minutes.

Acknowledgments

THERE ARE COUNTLESS PEOPLE who have touched my life over the years—the generations—through thick and thin... who have had a profound impact, whom God has used to shower me with blessing after blessing. Any endeavor to recount them all would certainly be incomplete; you *know* who you are, and I thank you.

Still, it is important to mention a few, without whom this volume would not have been possible. You have been a blessing to me, and you have my eternal gratitude.

— A.W.S.

Special thanks to:

DON & JULIE —

Our new family: your beautiful hearts, your prayers, and dedication made this work possible.

MY SISTERS, DARNELLE AND DARNETTE —

There is no way I could have done any of this without you. Really.

MY HUSBAND, LARRY —

Thank you for your patience and love.

JOHN, LEAH, & RICHARD —

Thank you for your timely advice, support, and faithfulness through the years.

CECIL —

Thank you for always coming to our rescue.

TIM & KIM —

For your continued prayers over the years, and all of the other blessings you have brought our way.

Index

A

B

C

D

E

F

G

H

J

K

L

M

N

O

P

Q

R

S

T

V

W

Z

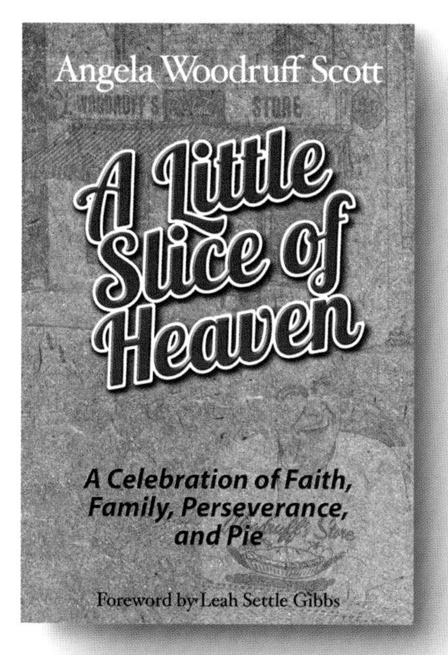

A Little Slice of Heaven

Audacious Faith, LLC : Publishers

The Good Books People

www.GoodBooks.us

MO
3297